Cambridge Elements ≡

Elements in Criminology
edited by
David Weisburd
George Mason University and Hebrew University of Jerusalem

USING THE POLICE CRAFT TO IMPROVE PATROL OFFICER DECISION-MAKING

James J. Willis
George Mason University

Heather Toronjo
George Mason University

T0311504

CAMBRIDGE
UNIVERSITY PRESS

Shaftesbury Road, Cambridge CB2 8EA, United Kingdom

One Liberty Plaza, 20th Floor, New York, NY 10006, USA

477 Williamstown Road, Port Melbourne, VIC 3207, Australia

314–321, 3rd Floor, Plot 3, Splendor Forum, Jasola District Centre, New Delhi – 110025, India

103 Penang Road, #05–06/07, Visioncrest Commercial, Singapore 238467

Cambridge University Press is part of Cambridge University Press & Assessment, a department of the University of Cambridge.

We share the University's mission to contribute to society through the pursuit of education, learning and research at the highest international levels of excellence.

www.cambridge.org
Information on this title: www.cambridge.org/9781009476003

DOI: 10.1017/9781009314534

First published 2023

A catalogue record for this publication is available from the British Library

ISBN 978-1-009-47600-3 Hardback
ISBN 978-1-009-31450-3 Paperback
ISSN 2633-3341 (online)
ISSN 2633-3333 (print)

Cambridge University Press & Assessment has no responsibility for the persistence or accuracy of URLs for external or third-party internet websites referred to in this publication and does not guarantee that any content on such websites is, or will remain, accurate or appropriate.

Using the Police Craft to Improve Patrol Officer Decision-Making

Elements in Criminology

DOI: 10.1017/9781009314534
First published online: December 2023

James J. Willis
George Mason University

Heather Toronjo
George Mason University

Author for correspondence: James J. Willis, jwillis4@gmu.edu

Abstract: In this Element we build on our previous work conceptualizing a craft learning model for governing police discretion. We envision a model for harnessing patrol officers' craft knowledge and skills, learned through experience handling similar street-level encounters over time, to the development of standards for evaluating the quality of their decision-making. To clarify the logic of this model and its potential for police reform, we situate it within the context of other systems of discretion control, including law, bureaucracy, science, and the community. We also consider obstacles. We conclude that police organizations need to balance the different strategies for channeling and controlling discretion toward the goal of advancing more transparent and principled decision-making. The challenge is finding a balance that helps prevent arbitrary, pernicious, or uncompromising uses of police authority, but that also empowers and rewards officers for using the skills of perception and resourcefulness that contribute to wise judgment.

Keywords: Discretion, craft, bureaucracy, reform, policing

ISBNs: 9781009476003 (HB), 9781009314503 (PB), 9781009314534 (OC)
ISSNs: 2633-3341 (online), 2633-3333 (print)

Contents

Given the significance of police discretion for the allocation of justice within American society, it is crucial to understand what determines the routine choices patrolmen make.

Michael K. Brown, *Working the Street* (1981)

Correct prognoses will generally issue from the judgements of those with better knowledge of mankind.

Can one learn this knowledge? Yes; some can. Not, however, by taking a course in it, but through *'experience'*.—Can someone else be a man's teacher in this? Certainly. From time to time he gives him the right *tip*.—This is what 'learning' and 'teaching' are like here.—

What one acquires here is not a technique; one learns correct judgements. There are also rules, but they do not form a system, and only experienced people can apply them right. Unlike calculating-rules.

What is most difficult here is to put this indefiniteness, correctly and unfalsified, into words.

Ludwig Wittgenstein, *Philosophical Investigations* (1958)
(as quoted by Nussbaum 1992, p. 54)

1 Introduction

The enormous discretionary authority of patrol officers operating at the "coal-face" of policing received little scholarly attention until the 1950s, when the American Bar Foundation Survey of the Administration of Criminal Justice conducted the first major observational study of criminal justice practitioners in the field (Walker 1992; Bayley 2008, p. 13). Researchers, riding along with patrol officers in cities and rural communities across three states, learned that police work was complex, and that officers did not simply act as ministerial agents of the law "doing precisely what they were mandated by law to do" (Goldstein 1977, p. 93). Instead, they also routinely exercised their authority in more informal ways with little guidance or oversight (Kelling 1999). According to police historian Samuel Walker (1992, pp. 56–57), this field research had a compelling effect on the researchers: "It was not only that innumerable routine decisions had profound implications for individuals, but also that these decisions were guided by no formal standards and were largely ad hoc accommodations designed "to get the job done." In the process, the members of the team also observed a great deal of lawlessness, racism, and casual unprofessional conduct."

Similar concerns about the pervasiveness and arbitrariness of discretion on the front lines were raised a decade later, amidst the Civil Rights movement of the 1960s. The National Advisory Commission on Civil Disorder (1968) reported on demonstrations against police brutality, institutional racism, and economic inequality (Cobb 2021). Around the same time, President Lyndon

Johnson's Commission on Law Enforcement and the Administration of Justice (1967, pp. 10, 103) recognized the "hard choices policemen must make every day," choices that depended largely on an individual police officer's personal discretion since "every policeman, however complete or sketchy his education, is an interpreter of the law."

Fifty years on, there is still much progress to be made. Police agencies and officers continue to gloss over, or deny (at least formally), the enormous leeway they have to choose "among possible causes of action or inaction" (Klockars 1985, p. 93). Moreover, the idea that police primarily act as law enforcers still exerts a strong grip on the public imagination. And yet with disturbing regularity, news stories and social media accounts describe troubling and tragic uses of police discretion in the form of unlawful police killings, controversial arrests, unjustified stops and searches, and reckless pursuits. The growing recognition that police officers may be "out of control" (Goldstein 1979, p. 239), neither protecting nor serving (Baldwin 1966), has led to the rise of Black Lives Matter, widespread protests, civil lawsuits, and national demands for police reform.

As others have argued, reckless or malignant abuses of police authority deserve to be central to efforts to improve policing (Thacher 2016, p. 535). However, reformers also need to wrestle with the full extent of patrol officers' discretionary leeway, the conditions that underlie it, and with formulating more innovative and effective mechanisms for structuring and governing its use. Even the most routine police–civilian encounters can involve factors that make these interactions nuanced, ambiguous, and complex. Egon Bittner, one of policing's most sophisticated observers, helped illustrate some of these challenges with several fine-grained analyses of the challenging situational judgments required in relation to seemingly low-profile encounters, such as patrol officers handling residents on skid-row (1967), responding to people with mental illness (1967a), managing complaints about a dog bite (1990, pp. 181–182), and telling groups of youths to "vacate a street corner" (1990, p. 187). The choices patrol officers make in these kinds of situations often do not "directly involve a decision whether or not to enforce a law" (Goldstein 1977, p. 95), but they can contribute to some of the most serious issues facing police–community relations today, including questionable uses of police authority, disproportionately harsh responses to petty offenses, and the indifferent or arbitrary treatment of community members, even when they are calling on the police for help and support.

High-profile and dramatic encounters may be the most likely to make national headlines, but most police activities do not involve crime fighting, making arrests, or using coercive force (Bittner 1990, pp. 240–243; Bayley 1994). A much larger proportion of patrol work can comprise numerous less visible but ambiguous situations, such as handling harassment complaints, arbitrating or mediating between disputants, responding to public disturbances, or "protecting the rights of individuals to live where they want to live and say what they want to say" (Goldstein 1967, p. 1125).

As Bittner (1990, p. 240) observes, "the activity of criminal law enforcement is not at all characteristic of day-to-day, ordinary occupational practices of the vastly preponderant majority of policemen." The Police Services Study conducted in the 1970s examined 26,418 calls for service in three metropolitan areas. It found that only 19 percent of calls involved crime, and only 2 percent involved violent crime (Walker and Katz 2005, p. 7). A recent and much larger analysis of millions of calls for service across nine agencies helps reveal the tremendous range of issues the police are called upon to handle, the majority of which do not involve criminal law enforcement, nor do they often result in officers taking any formal action (62–83 percent of calls received) (Lum, Koper, and Wu 2021, pp. 16–17). Currently, neither the law nor police administrators offer much guidance on most of the "mind-boggling variety" of police duties (Bittner 1990, p. 250), and unlike criminal incident or arrest reports, official record systems often fail to capture information on what actually transpired during many police–civilian encounters. Consequently, "what ultimately gets done depends primarily on the individual officer's perspicacity, judiciousness, and initiative," with few systems in place for assessing the patrol officer's actions as part of a regular process for strengthening performance accountability, or for improving decision-making in future encounters (Bittner 1990, p. 262; see also Goldstein 1977, p. 97).

There also appears to be muted interest among police administrators, supervisors, and line officers in reflecting upon and discussing these decisions, despite the current spotlight on the police. And yet research suggests that when it comes to "policing for people" (Mastrofski 1999), members of the public have high expectations for the quality of individual police service they feel they deserve (Goldstein 1977, p. 161; Mastrofski 1996; Tyler 2004). These expectations only seem to be increasing over time, as people capture and share details of their own interactions with police officers (or those of others), and upload their cell phone videos to various social media and websites (Bayley 2016). There can be little doubt that civilians are quite comfortable observing and judging how rightfully or reasonably they feel treated (Meares, Tyler, and Gardener 2015). Moreover, undesirable outcomes and widespread community outrage can result from what initially appear to be commonplace incidents, such as minor traffic violations, but that quickly escalate. It is possible that these outcomes could have been avoided by officers "slowing down," that is by paying careful attention to situational details of the immediate problem, and by doing the little things that help civilians feel respected and valued (and indeed respecting and valuing civilians), while not letting routineness and familiarity become a cause of undue complacency (Owens et al. 2018, p. 48).

Notwithstanding their importance, police responses to these encounters, which are more aligned with the police role as guardians of the community than warriors against crime (Rahr and Rice 2015), do not receive the attention they deserve, are rarely a central element of reform movements, and yet would seem to be crucial to improving community satisfaction, trust, and police legitimacy (Tyler 2004). Instead, reformers tend to focus on more sweeping organizational strategies, such as community- or problem-oriented policing, and grander objectives for transforming, or even abolishing, police organizations (Bittner 1970, p. 40; Mastrofski 1999, p. 1; Searcey 2020). Thus, a core question for advocates of police reform, one rendered more urgent by recent events, is what might be done to channel more principled and defensible everyday uses of police discretion, and to hold patrol officers more accountable for what they do and how well they do it?

To these ends, in this Element we build on some of our previous work (Willis, Koen, and Toronjo 2022; Willis and Toronjo 2023) to advance a *craft learning model* for reviewing and channeling officer decision-making. We see our model as a potential supplement to existing systems of discretion control, systems that may be marginalized by the powerful effects of the police subculture, and that can fall short in providing useful guidance in relation to the realities of actual police practice (Mastrofski 2000; Thacher 2008).

Our purpose is to envision a means for involving patrol officers more directly in the development of performance standards based on their considerable resource of collective, concrete, context-dependent knowledge and skills learned through their many and varied experiences working the street (Brown 1981; Flyvbjerg and Sampson 2001). Furthermore, we argue for a direct role for the public and other relevant experts or partners in helping improve street-level police discretion. While the problems of policing are not new, it seems a growing segment of the public may no longer be satisfied with delegating this responsibility to politicians and police managers. In developing our model, we are motivated by a desire to elevate policing as a "true" profession (Mastrofski 2000, p. 428), and we draw selectively on insights from some of the better-established professions, such as medicine and social work. One of the key characteristics of any profession is that its members are trusted to exercise their own judgment, and yet policing seems to lag behind in this respect.

By narrowing the potentially overwhelming array of criteria for assessing an officer's performance in a particular situation to some of the most relevant and practicable considerations, we argue that standards could offer useful guidance on how to exercise discretionary authority in everyday encounters with the public, contribute to the development of professional knowledge, and lead to more principled decision-making. As with any profession, there is a place for knowledge gained through scientific experimentation. There are medication efficacy trials in medicine, program evaluations in social work, studies of the deterrent effect of sentencing practices in law, just to name a few. But in policing, as in other professions, such science can only inform, not solve, the challenge of situationally and normatively complex problems (Lum and Koper 2017). We argue that officers also need frequent opportunities to develop their capacity for making skillful judgments by reflecting on specific cases, especially when they confront situations that are dynamic and unclear, and deciding what to do is not obvious.

For Bittner, good patrol work requires an ability to make subtle or deft judgments based on an intuitive grasp of situational exigencies, qualities and skills that need to be "liberated and allowed to take their proper place in the scheme of police organization" (Bittner 1990, pp. 146–147). Gary Klein (2011, p. 6), a proponent of naturalistic decision-making (NDM) (choices that occur in an unstructured and unpredictable social environment) refers to this as thinking and deciding in the "world of shadows, the world of ambiguity." To be effective, we further suggest that these standards need to be integrated with a compliance or accountability process for reviewing and assessing the choices made, both good and bad, and for encouraging the kind of honest and constructive feedback that promotes reflection and learning (Thacher 2001; Stoughton, Alpert, and Noble 2015).

The model we envision here is structured around a regular performance review process conducted by first-line supervisors to promote the kind of thoughtful deliberation that could aid "the exercise of proper discretion" (Goldstein 1963, p. 147). Building on recent interest in pushing policing to become a more critically reflective practice (Charles 2000; Ramsey 2014; Christopher 2015; Phelps et al. 2016), and on research suggesting that nonstandard supervisory interventions encouraging officers to reflect on their thought processes and actions can result in salutary effects (Owens et al. 2018), we outline a process that would involve supervisors regularly reviewing their officers' body-worn camera (BWC) footage through an interactive practitioner-based learning approach of reflection-in-action.

These prospects of guidance and control that we outline for the craft learning model are consistent with a post-bureaucratic focus on more flexible and transparent public service organizations (Thacher 2022). This focus encourages frontline workers to take initiative to address recurrent challenges or problems, but it also demands "that such initiative be reflective and accountable" (Sabel and Simon 2016, p. 167). This is in stark contrast to the current dominant paradigm in policing of increased administrative rulemaking and bureaucratization. This model, which rose to prominence in the mid-twentieth century (Mastrofski and Willis 2010), depends on "stable, hierarchically promulgated rules and lightly supervised discretion" and shows no signs of abating (Sabel and Simon 2016, p. 167).

What we propose is ambitious, especially because of its direct involvement of lower-level organizational participants in promoting fairer and more effective policing, the very same group that is considered responsible for much that currently ails policing, and because we seek to loosen police organizations' traditional, bureaucratic, and hierarchical "coercive-alienative" approach to strengthening compliance. We think that more attention should be paid to a "normative-moral" perspective, with its emphases on collaborative learning and strengthening the moral commitment between the community and the police toward good police work (Etizoni 1975, pp. 12–13; Mastrofski and Greene 1993).

While audacious, our proposal embraces the goals of the Elements' series, which promises "to focus on radical new ways of understanding and framing criminology, whether of place, communities, persons, or situations." Similar to John Laub's Presidential Address to the American Society of Criminology in 2003 (2004), we are suggesting the need for a "turning point" in the ideas around police reform, a turn which would focus more interest on the complex situational and normative dimensions of frontline police decision-making and on meaningful attempts to help officers "refine" their capacity "to humanely manage difficult incidents during the moments when they arise" (Thacher 2008, 2022, p. 64). Thus, we hope our Element will be a catalyst for building knowledge about the daily choices police officers are called upon to make, and for developing and testing new strategies for improving frontline decision-making processes and outcomes.

This Element begins by reviewing the current subsystems for controlling street-level discretion in police organizations. Doing so provides a context for understanding the logic of the craft learning model, and for assessing its potential for improving how patrol officers choose particular goals and tactics in their encounters with the public, and the values their actions implicate. We will pay particular attention to contrasting the recent resurgence of interest in the more constraining properties of the "if–then provisions in rules and procedures" of policymaking, which are largely limited to restricting discretion and punishing wrongdoing (Engel and Worden 2003, p. 132). Our framework emphasizes broader standards that practitioners might *strive* to meet when making decisions. Incidentally, the strongly hierarchical and punitive model of police professionalism extends to the use of BWCs, where much attention has been paid to how BWCs can strengthen compliance with rules and policies and help deter use of force and police misconduct (Lum et al. 2020). In comparison, there has been much less exploration of how to use this technology as a learning tool for capturing and improving craft knowledge and skills (Willis and Mastrofski 2017; Willis 2022).

Next, we build on some of our own research to provide a detailed description and explanation of our conceptualization of a craft learning model, before considering some of the challenges to what we envision, including misalignment with traditional police culture, the limited role of first-line supervisors, lack of public input into discretionary decision-making, and conflicting values. We conclude by summarizing our main ideas, and by considering the need to balance different strategies for controlling discretion, particularly those between bureaucracy, craft, and science.

We argue that the challenge for researchers and police reformers is finding a balance that is mutually enhancing – one that helps prevent arbitrary responses and abuses of police authority, but that also allows for, and rewards, patrol officers for using the kind of "imagination and resourcefulness" associated with the best that the police craft has to offer (Goldstein 1977, p. 82). We do not think this is a zero-sum proposition, namely, that it is possible to increase the role of craft in advancing good police work without degrading science or bureaucracy. This might be achieved by encouraging a shared commitment to the "mutual aims and interests" of better policing (Mastrofski and Greene 1993, p. 83). Indeed, Lloyd Ohlin, a consultant for the field research on the original American Bar Foundation Survey, and a crucial advisor for the overall project, proposed a "middle course" to decision-making that supported "thoughtful discretion" by rewarding excellence and by allowing for flexibility and the exercise of "intelligent judgment." Such a course

> requires training in the decision-making that is guided by the basic values of a democratic society and professional norms of conduct. It also requires constructive use of supervision, review procedures, and policy development involving frontline decisionmakers. It calls for rules that do not take the form of mandated action but require attention to the criteria that should guide action and inform sensible judgments. The challenge is to devise controls that preserve and nurture that kind of discretion. (1993, p. 18)

2 Police Discretion and Strategies for Its Control

Since the American Bar Foundation called attention to the broad discretion enjoyed by patrol officers about seventy years ago, police leaders, public officials, and reformers have sought to structure and control it. In this section, we draw and expand upon the work of police scholar Stephen Mastrofski and others to examine policing's major discretion control strategies, many of which fall under one or more of the following five categories: (1) rule of law, (2) administrative rulemaking, (3) community participation, (4) police science, and (5) professional governance. These systems overlap, and understanding the challenges, opportunities, and consequences of a craft learning model first requires understanding the nature of these existing subsystems for influencing how policing gets done. The current policing crisis demonstrates how reformers continue to struggle with their effectiveness in trying to control the exercise of police authority and attain the 'Holy Grail of democratic policing' (Worden and Dole 2019).

2.1 The Rule of Law

According to the legal scholar H. M. Hart (1958, p. 402), the criminal law should not be treated abstractly, but examined as a method or "a way of doing something" in the real-life context of the institutions that make use of it and give it meaning. At the state level, legislators debate and enact criminal codes, and the judiciary is responsible for interpreting these codes and reviewing police conduct. From the perspective of the police, the law sets forth "technical standards and expectations that stipulate or guide the officer's actions in a number of domains" (Mastrofski et al. 2000, p. 313). The role of the law in guiding officer behavior tends to be "downplayed" by scholars (Herbert 1998, p. 352), who point to the powerful effects of the occupational subculture. Nonetheless, despite its limitations for effectively structuring discretion, "all basic police responsibilities and powers are defined by the law" (Herbert 1998, p. 352). Most obviously, the law instructs officers on the kinds of problems that deserve their attention, and the kinds of actions that are permissible. As Mastrofski (2000, p. 84) notes:

> Few would argue that the law is irrelevant to these decisions. It is clear that the law empowers police, giving them the authority to intervene and take certain actions (e.g., arrest) in specific circumstances (where evidence suggests the probability of a violation). Without a legal basis for intervention and action, it is undoubtedly true that the police would show less inclination to get involved in many problems and take certain legal actions.

In interpreting whether and how the law applies to a particular situation, officers must know its directives and evaluate what the evidence warrants. Thus, the law is fundamentally important for helping officers define a situation as meriting their attention, and for shaping their response (Harmon 2021). These empowering aspects of the law are illustrated in the many provisions of a state's motor vehicle code, which provides police with "a nearly unlimited reservoir of legal authority to pull motorists over when they want to check for fugitives and contraband (or, for that matter, when they want to pursue any other goal ancillary to the overt purpose of the traffic code)" (Thacher 2016, p. 103).

The fact that patrol officers will use the law as a resource to accomplish whatever objectives they identify as necessary helps explain why it is applied in ways that may appear to others to be arbitrary or legally inconsistent (Bittner 1990, p. 246; Mastrofski 2000). For example, the purpose of a traffic citation following a legal stop might be to raise revenues for the city, or to satisfy a department quota, rather than the ostensible purpose of punishing violators to increase traffic safety (Klockars 1985, p. 99). The stop might also be used to discriminate against specific groups, which is why some reformers have focused much of their attention on controlling police discretion through law's restraining properties, or its capacity for proscribing certain police actions. Some have argued that the law's greatest potential for influencing police behavior seems to lie "in its capacity to define forbidden actions . . . rather than to specify desired ones" (Mastrofski and Greene 1993, p. 84).

This variation and potential for abuse helps explain the motivational basis behind the 1960s "due process" revolution of the Warren Court era (1953–68). The Supreme Court under the leadership of Chief Justice Earl Warren helped establish standards for the legal control of the police regarding the appropriate basis for making an arrest, stopping and searching a civilian, and for interrogating those accused of committing a crime (Walker 1992). In *Mapp* v. *Ohio* (1961), the Court ruled that evidence collected in an illegal search and seizure was not admissible in court, and in *Miranda* v. *Arizona* (1966), police were required to inform detained criminal suspects of their rights before being interrogated to protect suspects from self-incrimination. The articulation of criminal procedural rights under the Constitution is closely tied to a long history of racial discrimination in the United States and the Court's concern with fairness and equality (Skogan and Frydl 2004, p. 254). Research, however, shows that police are quite capable of using their discretion to circumvent legal prescriptions and that a system which relies upon a miniscule proportion of questionable cases being reviewed in court to be effective is a relatively weak form of accountability (Gould and Mastrofski 2004). Victims of unfair police practices are unlikely to make a complaint, and officers rarely file charges against each other. Even if a case makes it to the prosecutor's office, it will often get screened before it gets to any judge (Mastrofski 2000, p. 424).

Scholars have suggested several other limitations to the law as a formal system of discretion control. Laws are written in very general terms, leaving officers with considerable leeway in choosing how to apply them. Even when it comes to laws designed to specifically narrow an officer's decision-making (e.g., mandatory arrest laws), officers must still decide whether the factors relevant to a specific domestic violence assault meet required legal standards for an arrest. That is, even these highly targeted laws "do not eliminate the exercise of discretion .... Was there in fact an assault? Was it a felonious assault? How serious is that injury?" (Walker 1993, p. 38). There still remains much room for interpretation, particularly when it comes to misdemeanor offenses (Mastrofski 2000, p. 423).

While it could be argued that a facet of late modernity is the rapid expansion of substantive criminal law to cover many areas of social life, "the law fails even to recognize most of the discretionary choices open to police and therefore provides no guidance on what to do when an arrest cannot be made" (Mastrofski 2000, p. 423). In the case of the neighbor dispute in an apartment building that we introduce in Section 3 (where both parties have strongly opposed viewpoints), it is not clear a law has even been violated that would permit an arrest. In general, when there is little ground for a legal arrest, the law offers police little guidance: "the criminal law devotes virtually all of its attention to arrest, offering scarcely more than a whisper on banishment (except for protection from abuse orders), and nothing about threats, warnings, advice, and persuasion" (Mastrofski et al. 2000, p. 313). With the scenario of the estranged neighbors, should the officers separate the parties, counsel them together, threaten them, call a family member, or refer them to the building manager?

In sum, the law itself and the external legal institutions designed to strengthen compliance with its edicts are important influences on police decision-making, but there are still significant limits on their effectiveness as a mechanism of guidance and control. In light of this, since the 1960s, many reformers have advocated for an internal system of administrative rulemaking that tries to regulate police decision-making through more detailed department rules, regulations, and policies, and through the use of internal reviews to help ensure patrol officer compliance.

2.2 Administrative Rulemaking

By the mid-1970s administrative rulemaking had become the dominant paradigm for controlling police discretion, and it remains so today (Walker 1993).

Herman Goldstein (1967), one of the original members of the American Bar Foundation team, and Kenneth Culp Davis (1969, 1975), an administrative law scholar, played important roles in the rise of this paradigm. Others, such as Joseph Goldstein (1963), reacted in dismay to the American Bar Foundation's finding that police officers were usurping the legislative branch of government by failing to enforce the laws as written. He demanded that discretion be considered illegal and abolished. In contrast, Herman Goldstein recognized that discretion was an inevitable feature of police work (certainly the police did not have the resources to enforce every law) and was best managed through written administrative policies (Walker 1993a, p. 39). The latter perspective prevailed, whereby police executives are responsible for articulating detailed rules and regulations that help define, clarify, and restrict police discretion, and for implementing rigorous accountability mechanisms for their enforcement. The importance of accreditation by CALEA (the Commission on Accreditation for Law Enforcement Accreditation) as an indicator of police professionalism is an illustration of the value the police and others afford this approach. As part of the accreditation process, CALEA puts significant weight on agencies implementing policies written by subject area experts and on evidence of compliance (Abner and Rush 2022). Similarly, policy and oversight are identified as the second pillar of reform by the recent President's Taskforce on Twenty-First Century Policing (2015).

The administrative rulemaking model's focus on the development and implementation of formal policies and procedures to control discretion is consistent with key elements of the bureaucratic or paramilitary model of police organization designed to help an agency channel its efforts toward the accomplishment of key goals and interests (Willis, Mastrofski, and Weisburd 2004). These include hierarchical differentiation (a rank structure delineating the chain of command), formalization (written rules prescribing procedures and practices), and centralization (where the locus of decision-making authority is located at the top of the hierarchy and accountability flows up the chain of command) (Mastrofski and Ritti 2000).

Because criminal laws are written so generally, more detailed department guidelines are supposed to help "channel discretion in ways that further the law's intent and that are practicable from the officer's point of view" (Mastrofski 2000, p. 426). There has been a recent resurgence of interest in this approach to advancing police reform (Friedman 2017; White, Fradella, and Flippin 2020). Indeed, stringent guidelines and accountability structures were key features of the *George Floyd Justice in Policing Act of 2021* reform bill.

Administrative rulemaking is an important means of regulation and compliance, but it also has some key limitations (Krantz 1979; Walker 1993;

Ponomarenko 2019). Patrol officers make decisions in varied situations that are unique and unpredictable. In organizational terms, police work occurs in a task environment that is heterogeneous, and where the 'technology' for getting things done is poorly developed (Mastrofski and Ritti 2000). Put differently, the idiosyncrasies of street-level encounters and the demands they put on decision-makers are not well understood, nor is the technical capacity of the police for producing desirable outcomes (Engel and Worden 2003).

These features present significant challenges to an administrative rulemaking model that uses a top-down approach to control discretion through the enforcement of general bureaucratic rules (Bittner 1983). It is difficult developing regulations sufficiently plentiful for the extraordinarily diverse situations that officers are called upon to handle, and that are capable of covering the many factors relevant to an officer's decision (Bittner 1990; Mastrofski 2000). Policies that try to create rules around all this complexity can become inflexible and cumbersome and, even when detailed, "may remain obtuse in the face of the unpredictable circumstances that continue to arise" (Thacher 2020, p. 756). This helps explain why administrative reviews are evoked selectively, often as a formal disciplinary process focused on rule compliance in relation to civilian complaints, or in relation to relatively rare critical incidents, particularly deadly force (and more recently the use of nonlethal force), domestic violence, and high-speed pursuits (Walker 1993).

Moreover, the rulemaking model tends not to afford much importance to the valuable "resources of knowledge, skill, and judgment" that experience teaches patrol officers and that constitute the craft of police work (Goldstein 1967, p. 1123; Bittner 1983; Sklansky and Marks 2008; Willis 2013). And yet research suggests that based on their hands-on experience, some patrol officers have developed a level of artistry in their work that is hard to ignore (Willis and Mastrofski 2017). Muir's (1977) professional police officer is capable of handling complex situations with uncanny skill, and Bittner (1967) describes a set of adroit techniques that allow patrol officers to make prudent judgments when keeping the peace on skid row. At its best, the domain of an officer's professional competence in dealing with the "indeterminacies and value conflicts of practice" (Schön 1983, p. 19) including "making good arrests, deescalating crises, investigating crimes, using coercion and language effectively, abiding by the law and protecting individual rights, developing knowledge of the community, and imparting a sense of fairness to one's actions" (Mastrofski 1988, p. 65). This is not to romanticize police expertise as a "privileged, divine-like attribute" (Lvovsky 2021, p. 4), but to simply recognize the potential benefits of systematically accessing the kind of craft or professional knowledge that is unavailable to outsiders, who lack the same level of mastery or experience (Moore 1995; Thacher 2008).

Herman Goldstein (1979, p. 249) recognized the advantages of craft knowledge in his conceptualization of problem-oriented policing: "For the individualized practices of police officers and the vast amount of knowledge they acquire about the situations they handle, taken together, are an extremely rich resource that is too often overlooked by those concerned about improving the quality of police services."

Others thought very differently. Kenneth Davis, one of rulemaking's strongest advocates, explicitly *excluded* the knowledge of patrol officers when outlining the major elements of regulatory supervision. According to Davis (1975, p. 113), those aloft the police organization should be solely responsible for controlling discretion by writing detailed rules and procedures: as "top officers" they "obviously [had] the skills and broad understanding that patrolmen typically lack."

Last, bureaucratic rules generally establish minimum requirements for performance (Bittner 1983), fostering judgments of adequacy or "failures to do anything wrong." In this respect, they function differently to operative standards common to a wide range of other professional practices, such as teaching, nursing, and social work. The latter raise performance expectations by trying to articulate fine-grained distinctions between "good and bad work practices" (Bittner 1990, p. 146). At its best, craft or "workmanship" can establish expectations for skilled performance that far surpass those of general laws or policies (Bittner 1983; Klein 2011).

Some evidence suggests that newer versions of the administrative rulemaking model are opening up opportunities for police officers to share their street-level experiences during the review process to promote learning and improve decision-making (Thacher 2020). Still, attempts to combine the dual goals of experiential learning and rule-based compliance raise questions about their compatibility. Police agencies are punishment-centered bureaucracies (Gouldner 1954) whose existing review processes for strengthening internal accountability are better equipped for identifying and disciplining misconduct than promoting skilled performance (Bittner 1990; Mastrofski 2000). These control features of more traditional compliance-monitoring systems undermine efforts to encourage a low-risk and open-ended review process for facilitating learning about discretionary choices (Schön 1983).

For example, strict accountability can discourage efforts to search for, and experiment with, innovative, and potentially more effective, alternatives to standard police responses (Schön 1987, p. 4). The dominance of top-down management and coercion for gaining compliance can also alienate officers.

Sklansky (2008, p. 166) argues that "rigidly rule-bound workplaces are stulti-fying, demeaning" and can lead to the "distinctive sense of estrangement that police officers feel from society." This sense of alienation can help mitigate the influence of rules for controlling police officers' behavior, "which is therefore directed mostly toward giving only the appearance of compliance while actually subverting the objectives of formal law [*and policy*] and authority and avoiding punishment" (Mastrofski and Greene 1993, p. 83, italics added). Similarly, the authoritarian character of excluding patrol officers in the formulation of rules and strategies for compliance is contrary to the very democratic values which officers are supposed to be upholding: "values of openness, tolerance, and compromise; habits of engagement, cooperation, and deliberation" (Sklansky 2008, p. 168).

Despite their limitations, rules accompanied with strong disciplinary prac-tices, such as those associated with deadly force, use of force, and vehicle pursuits can be effective in shaping officer behavior (Walker 1993; Skogan and Frydl 2004; Walker and Archbold 2014). At the same time, their narrow focus on why an officer did or did not use force, engage in a pursuit, or make an arrest would seem to do little to help police agencies understand the many different facets of performance that people care about. They also appear less capable of improving a key feature of the quality of patrol officer decision-making – a capacity to make sophisticated situational judgments highly dependent on context: "It may be that this crucial dimension of police discretion cannot be expressed in an administrative policy, any more than a physician's diagnostic or therapeutic discretionary judgment can be reduced to the pages of a medical text book" (Klockars 1985, p. 113).

2.3 Community Participation

The crises of the 1960s, which helped shape the Warren Court Era, also influenced the rise of community policing over the next three decades. Public disappointment at unresponsive and overly bureaucratic police agencies led reformers to find ways to give community members "more participation in and influence over decision-making" (Mastrofski 2019, p. 56). This is a core elem-ent of the community policing reform movement, which requires that police agencies engage frequently with the public to identify community norms and sentiments that help "establish policies and develop practices" (Skogan 2019, p. 28). It is worth noting that community policing shares this desire for greater community input into police matters with the administrative rulemaking model of discretion control. Under administrative rulemaking, policies that are subject to criticism and revision by the public before being vetted will be improved.

Advocates of this approach also suggest that another benefit of opening up the rulemaking process to the public is that it helps people better understand and more fully appreciate the complexities of policing. Simple platitudes about the police as crime fighters, or unrealistic expectations about what the police can accomplish (what Bittner (1990, p. 91) referred to sardonically as "programmatic idealizations"), foster cynicism and do little to promote realistic reform.

From a community policing perspective, avenues for community influence on police discretion can take many forms. Researchers have focused on the more formal aspects of this: police–community partnership, including beat meetings, changes to formal organizational structures (e.g., organizational decentralization), and civilian review boards. Beat meetings in local neighborhoods between the police and those who live or work in the area are designed to help police identify priorities and suitable tactics to address them (Skogan 2019). In these venues, community members should have the opportunity to share information, discuss the kinds of local problems that traditionally have not been the focus of police attention (e.g., physical disorder), and engage in problem-solving partnerships for enhancing public safety. The assumption that those best equipped to address local problems are those who confront them most regularly implies that decision-making should be decentralized to sergeants and individual patrol officers assigned to fixed geographic areas (Skogan 2019, p. 35). Community policing emphasizes that officers should be trusted to use their best judgment in helping resolve the problems in the communities to which they have been assigned (Mastrofski 1988).

The demands for greater community input include the creation of civilian review boards. These can take different forms, including being fully or partially staffed by nonpolice, and they vary in terms of their powers, but they are generally given access to police files to investigate individual complaints and make recommendations to the chief executive. Their focus is on officer wrongdoing, and their actions are guided by specific rules for reviewing cases and for ensuring that the procedural rights of officers are respected (Walker 2016, p. 633).

In comparison to police–community partnerships, problem-solving, and civilian review boards, the more direct effects of community policing on the judgments that officers make in everyday street encounters have garnered less attention. What we do know is that the link between community policing attitudes and police behavior has been "quite modest" in size and has not stimulated a radical shift in the "form or practice of police work" (Mastrofski 2019, pp. 53, 55). Past assessments have shown that pro-community policing officers were more likely to act in ways consistent with procedural justice (Mastrofski, Snipes, and Supina 1996), but that community policing specialists in two police agencies were less likely to spend time in face-to-face encounters to learn about community members and their problems (Parks et al. 1999). Moreover, there is some evidence that a disposition toward community policing can lead to troubling uses of police discretion. In field observations of one department, officers who were most strongly committed to community policing were also those who were most likely to commit search and seizures that violated civilians' constitutional rights (Gould and Mastrofski 2004).

One explanation for the limited influence of the community on patrol officers' situational judgments is that people have been willing to defer to the professional judgment of the police as experts (Mastrofski and Greene 1993, p. 88). Thus, community input has not extended to "basic police department operations, such as patrol" (Walker 2016, p. 645). Unsurprisingly, there has been little police interest in changing this expectation by creating mechanisms for soliciting detailed input on the specific actions of police officers in their routine encounters, and by providing an opportunity for community members to ask questions and hear an explanation for an officer's choices.

Thus, the tenets of community policing might have pushed police executives to acknowledge the broad discretionary powers of police officers, but they have stimulated less interest in how these powers might be better governed. For example, under a community policing model, patrol officers are expected to address minor incidents of social and physical disorder that undermine neighborhood livability (Skogan 2006), and to take their cues from community norms about what are acceptable or unacceptable behaviors and responses to them (Wilson and Kelling 1982). These norms are often ambiguous and subject to multiple interpretations. Consequently, attempts to identify and protect them can take different forms, and yet police administrators have been slow to provide practical guidance on what order maintenance policing activities actually involve (Thacher 2004).

In sum, community contributions to guiding and reforming street-level decision-making has been modest. All of this raises the following question, one that we consider as part of the craft learning model: What would be an appropriate form of community engagement and accountability when it comes to the choices officers make in police–public encounters, one that is not simply limited to coordinated problem-solving efforts and instances of police wrongdoing? It would seem that there is plenty of room for experimenting with methods for engaging the community and other relevant experts (e.g., mental health workers) to help strengthen "officers' skills in reducing misjudgments" and to help ensure that "the police are in possession of the requisite tools to maintain order, protect individual rights, and develop respect" (Mastrofski 1988, p. 56).

2.4 Police Science

Police science or evidence-based policing (EBP) is the most recent effort to help govern police officers' choices (Lum and Koper 2017). Evidence-based policing requires that "decision-making in policing be strongly influenced by basic and applied research" (Weisburd et al. 2023, p. 13), and it has gained considerable traction among policymakers since one of its staunchest advocates, Lawrence Sherman (1984, p. 61), remarked that "scientific experimentation holds the potential for revolutionizing police discretion." From the EBP perspective, police executives are responsible for ensuring that scientific methods and knowledge are key elements of police education and training, are integral to the management and operations of police organizations, and are features of line officer decision-making (Neyroud and Weisburd 2023). Some agencies might even have in-house "evidence cops" to monitor what the department is doing and to ensure that it is complying with evidence-based practices and guidelines (Sherman 1998).

Although EBP embraces a wide range of scientific methodologies and research topics, its scientific agenda puts particular value on the production of systematic, context-independent knowledge that contributes to explanation and prediction (Flyvbjerg and Sampson 2001, p. 27). Central to this approach are program evaluations using experimental and quasi-experimental research designs, which are intended to determine "what works" in reducing crime and disorder, increasing procedural justice, and improving other community outcomes.

A helpful illustration of the thrust of this EBP approach is the research conducted on the relationship between crime and place. Based on a series of rigorous studies, David Weisburd has suggested the law of crime concentration across cities where approximately less than 5 percent of street segments account for about 50 percent of crime (Weisburd 2015). The implication is that concentrating police resources at micro-places can help reduce crime, and rigorous program evaluations of hot spots policing programs consistently show that these can have statistically significant and short-term effects on crime outcomes without resulting in crime displacement (Braga and Weisburd 2020). A recent study concludes that when police officers are trained in procedural justice, hot spots policing can result in decreases in crime and increases in community satisfaction (Weisburd et al. 2022).

Although it has its critics (Sparrow 2011; Greene 2014; Thacher 2001, 2020), EBP's contributions seem clearest when it comes to generating the kind of generalizable knowledge that aids policymakers in choosing those police strategies or interventions which science suggests are most effective (Willis and

Toronjo 2019). Because of this conceptualization of police work, EBP advocates for the greater use of randomized controlled trials (RCTs) in policing (similar to the evidence-based movement in medicine). These trials are designed to minimize possible biases affecting scientific evidence that a policy causes desirable or undesirable results. In a randomized experiment "the effect of treatment is disentangled from the confounding effects of other factors" (Weisburd 2003, p. 338), making RCTs a powerful means for drawing conclusions about whether a particular program or treatment actually worked as intended.

A different view of the relationship between police work and professional knowledge, and the one advanced here as a supplement to EBP, puts greater emphasis on the complex situational nature of police judgments (Bittner 1970; Thacher 2008). Under conditions which are "dynamic, uncertain, and time compressed," and where multiple and subtle situational details might need to be taken into consideration, research suggests that decision-makers, such as fire commanders, nurses, and military personnel, rely heavily on their experiences or *context-dependent* knowledge (Alpert and Rojek 2011, p. 3). According to the NDM model, the benefits of applying universal rules and scientific generalizations are less clear in this kind of environment (Salas, Rosen, and DiazGranados 2010). This helps explain why police officers, while recognizing the merits of science, have been slow to embrace research and evidence as firm guides to action in their daily work (Telep and Lum 2014; Jonathan-Zamir et al. 2019). Rather, skilled decision-makers often rely on "artistic, intuitive processes" (Schön 1983, p. 49), which are based on extensive practice experiencing similar situations directly, or vicariously, over time. This enables them to recognize complex patterns, which are often processed with little conscious awareness (Kahneman and Klein 2009). Rather than making comparisons between alternatives, these are then matched to the current situation in order to identify an effective choice (Klein, Calderwood, and Clinton-Cirocco 2010). When there is not a match, the decision-maker continues to explore situational cues and seeks out additional information to make a reasoned decision (Klein 2011).

The implication of the NDM is that to build a capacity for intelligent judgment, you need to strengthen intuition by "building experiences that result in more accurate and comprehensive tacit knowledge" (Klein 2015, p. 166). In contrast to NDM, EBP treats intuition with greater suspicion because of the dangers of automated, implicit biases (Sherman 1998; Lum 2009), and because there is no guarantee that *experience* will necessarily translate into *expertise*. This is a fair criticism, but there is also evidence that proficient performers, unlike novices, rely less on context-independent rules and knowledge and more on features of the actual situation "to make perceptual discriminations, to recognize patterns, to draw on rich mental models, and to judge typicality" (Flyvbjerg and Sampson 2001; Klein 2015, p. 166). Consequently, NDM is less interested in teaching decision strategies created in artificial environments, preferring to have practitioners examine and reflect on complex cases, so they can accumulate and bring "to bear a richer and broader knowledge base and conceptual base for making intuitive judgments and decisions" (Klein 2015, p. 168).

Another distinguishing feature of street-level decision-making is that patrol officers must confront numerous complex and conflicting values or different "ends" worth accomplishing in a given situation (e.g., liberty, economy, dignity, just deserts) (Thacher 2001). Good police work requires that patrol officers are capable of making good moral judgments about the "right thing to do" in an encounter (Muir 1977; Mastrofski 2018). For example, in the case of a misdemeanor domestic assault, evidence and policy notwithstanding, a spouse might plead with a police officer not to arrest her husband for fear of being evicted, and for fear of having her children taken from her by child protective services. She might also refuse to testify against him. The right thing in this situation is by no means clear and uncontroversial.

Police administrators and scholars have generally been reluctant to engage directly with the unavoidable moral dimensions of police work. As Bayley and Bittner note (1984, p. 59): "Police have always tried to appear exclusively as technical agents of law rather than instruments of public morality." Fortunately, EBP is beginning to take more of an interest in the ethical and moral context of policing (Neyroud and Weisburd 2023), but what form this will take is not yet well developed. Moreover, following the example of Max Weber, some might be skeptical of a science-based approach for contributing to moral understanding. In his book on police discretion and the limits of reform, Michael Brown notes (1981, p. 295):

> Unlike most contemporary social scientists, Weber had a keen sense of the limits of science, of the questions it could not resolve. Science might provide one with factual and even causal knowledge, but it could never answer fundamental questions, those pertaining to what should be done. Yet it is precisely such moral issues that are at the core of the problem of discretion, and that a professional knowledge grounded in science cannot answer. Nor do we really want science to provide this kind of knowledge. The danger, as Weber feared, is that science and technology would encroach upon the realms of values and politics, and that political decisions would be made on the basis of scientific or pseudoscientific knowledge; or, perhaps worse, such knowledge would be used as a rationalization for decisions.

Others, however, appear more sanguine about the role social science can make to improving moral judgment. Some scholars, such as Bent Flyvbjerg (2012, p. 26), declare it to be social science's only role and recommend that social science "drop all pretense, however indirect, at emulating the success of the natural sciences in producing cumulative and predictive theory." Muir's (1977) use of close observation and interviews of patrol officers is an example of how research can help illuminate some of the moral and intellectual virtues that appear to contribute to good policing, including how these might be developed. Similarly, David Thacher (2006, 2020) has suggested that researchers can assist with identifying case studies and relevant normative theories, as part of a process of facilitating in-depth discussions around the value judgments that a specific case implicates. Thus, Thacher argues for a research model that combines empirical with normative inquiry to help police identify and interpret important public values, including acceptable trade-offs when they conflict, in ways that could help officers make more considered judgments.

Because of experimental research's focus on instrumental knowledge or the best means to an end (and not on the kind of practical knowledge necessary for examining and choosing between different ends), it can contribute to these kinds of debates but "it cannot speak to the full range of concerns relevant to criminal justice practice, which is characterized by a great variety and ambiguity of values" (Thacher 2001, p. 387). A similar observation has been made by Bent Flyvbjerg and Steven Sampson (2001, p. 58). Drawing on Aristotle's distinction between scientific knowledge (episteme) and technical knowledge (techne), they advocate for a phronetic approach to social science that uses case studies to help decision-makers analyze and interpret values in exercising judgment and making choices. According to Thacher and Rein (2004, p. 460), "'values' are the ultimate ends of public policy – the goals and objectives that policy aims to promote as desirable in their own right, not just as means to some other objective."

By helping to identify the likely outcome of an officer's actions, social science may be able to help officers learn about the effectiveness of specific tactics, or whether they produced unintended outcomes. However, to be more useful to police practice, police science needs to better meet the interests of patrol officers by shifting more of its attention toward evaluating the tacit knowledge that surrounds the actual "operational imperatives of the work that police officers do" (Bayley and Bittner 1984, p. 47). Thus, it could benefit by apportioning more of its focus to understanding what science can learn from the different police tactics or "treatment options" that officers' experiences suggest are best matched to the complexities of a given set of circumstances, and by considering how these might be tested (Mastrofski and Uchida 1993; Willis

2013; Willis and Mastrofski 2018). For Bayley and Bittner (1984, p. 53), "only rigorous testing of the efficacy of tactical choices can at last transform police lore into the wisdom its practitioners think it to be." Moreover, to more fully account for the challenges of street-level police work, it could consider forms of empirical inquiry that help identify the values that powerfully shape police decision-making and help illuminate the complexities of how these values are interpreted and understood. When science fails to pursue an "adequate conception" of what the ends of policing should look like, it is in danger of losing its "vitality and purpose" (Thacher 2004, p. 180).

2.5 Professional Governance

The final discretion control system is the occupational culture, or the common set of values, norms, attitudes, and beliefs that lend meaning to how members of a profession view each other and outsiders, and the tasks they do (Loftus 2010; Mastrofski and Willis 2010). Coercion lies at the core of the police culture, and the pressures that accompany the capacity to use force give rise to many of the themes "interwoven" into officers' attitudes and beliefs (Mastrofski 2000, p. 417). While the police culture is not monolithic (Paoline 2003), ethnographers have identified some of its common elements as the uncertainty of police work, isolation and suspicion toward outsiders, mutual dependency, and a sense among patrol officers that "no matter what they do somebody will find fault" (Brown 1981, p. 49; Mastrofski and Willis 2010). Other features of the occupational culture include conservative politics and morality, and the celebration of a strong masculine perspective valorizing courage, strength, and honor (Loftus 2010).

Advocates of reform frequently anticipate resistance from the traditional police culture and its warrior outlook (Rahr and Rice 2015; Willis and Mastrofski 2017) and consider ways that these might be overcome (President's Task Force 2015). Less attention has been paid to learning what police officers value about their work, what constitutes its quality, how best to achieve it, and how best to avoid low quality. Other than the work of a few scholars (Muir 1977; Bayley and Bittner 1984; Bittner 1990; Herbert 1998; Willis and Mastrofski 2017), patrol officers' views on the craft elements of their work remain understudied. Herbert's (1998, p. 358) observation, made over twenty years ago, that craft (the "normative order of competence") was the least understood of police officers' cultural outlooks still pertains today.

While the police might contend that craft expertise should help elevate policing to a similar status as other professions, such as law, medicine, engineering, accounting, or social work, this is not likely to convince others

(Brown 1981). Police officers may meet a profession's formal criterion of being members of an occupation by putting the public's needs beyond their own, and by holding themselves to a professional code of ethics, but they fall short on several other key attributes of what it means to be a true "professional" (Brown 1981, pp. 40–41; Mastrofski 2000). Policing cannot yet claim authority that is based on a body of sophisticated knowledge that has been empirically validated. Moreover, while the length of pre-service training and level of education required for police officers has increased in terms of its length and complexity (Skogan and Frydl 2004, p. 142), it still falls far short of what is required for doctors and lawyers (Sloan and Paoline 2021). Most police departments do not require a college degree, nor is there the granting of a license to practice.

Furthermore, policing has not yet developed standards for evaluating performance through a combination of experiential and scientific knowledge. Nor has it found ways to apply these standards in ways that help guide everyday judgements, and to subject these judgments to a more systematic and critical evaluation by other members of the profession (other key attributes of professionalism).

This helps explain why scholars have tended to use the term "police professionalism" differently to how the term professional is generally applied to an occupation, namely, to refer to police reformers' efforts, rooted in Progressivism, to promote efficiency and accountability through administrative rulemaking and bureaucratization (Kelling and Moore 1988; Sklansky 2008, p. 37). Requiring that patrol officers make judgments according to the dictates of bureaucracy, science, and the law is, of course, the opposite to what real professionalism demands, which is the freedom to make decisions based on one's own expertise (Mastrofski 2000, p. 429). Certainly, an officer's judgment can be informed by these other systems for trying to rationalize and routinize police work (Brown 1981), but it cannot be reduced to them because of police work's unavoidably improvisational and interpretative qualities. Flyvbjerg and Sampson (2001, p. 19) provide a useful analogy for illuminating the value of experience, intuition, and interpretation in making these practical decisions while attending to a large number of complex and ambiguous situational details:

> Take something as mundane as riding a bicycle. How could we, for example, "teach" the difference between nearly falling and the need to learn over in order to turn a corner? How do we explain the best response to being off balance? Bicyclists can bicycle because they have the necessary know-how, achieved via practical experiences, invariably accompanied by a few childhood scrapes and bruises. Experience cannot necessarily be verbalized, intellectualized, and made into rules.

The small literature on this professional "know-how" that police officers think they learn as "possessors of an art that can be learned only by experience" (Wilson 1968, p. 283) can be organized around three key elements: knowledge, skill, and judgment.

Bayley and Bittner (1984) assert that the accomplishment of certain goals frames the occupation's understanding of skilled police work: meeting department norms (including confirming to bureaucratic regulations), containing violence and controlling disorder, preventing crime, avoiding physical injury, and not provoking the public to retaliate in career-threatening ways. Based on his observations of police, Mastrofski (1996) adds problem resolution, problem identification, lawfulness of police response, and economy in police response as additional goals. In an empirical study on the elements of craft, many of these were identified by patrol officers as top priorities in traffic stops and domestic disputes (common and challenging situations), as were following rules and matching a response to the seriousness of the violation (Willis and Mastrofski 2017). Reducing future citizen complaints and saving police time/effort were ranked lowest. Others, such as law enforcement leaders, including Charles Ramsey and Sue Rahr (Ramsey 2014; Rahr and Rice 2015), take a broader view and identify protecting individuals' constitutional rights and acting as community guardians as the main goals of police work.

The tactical choices available to officers to help achieve these goals are extensive, which helps explain variation in officers' responses (Bayley 1986). Officers, however, are quite comfortable assessing one another's performance, and more experienced officers will often express a preference for one tactical alternative over another in a specific set of circumstances (Bayley and Bittner 1984, p. 45). In making decisions, the traditional view of the police culture puts high value on the acquisition of detailed knowledge of particular people and places, and the history of events (Bittner 1967; Muir 1977).

Some observational research suggests that those police officers identified as experts by their peers behave differently than average officers in potentially violent encounters, being more likely to take charge and showing greater versatility in their tactical choices (Bayley and Garofalo 1989). To the extent that these differences result in effective and efficient decision-making, they are consistent with studies suggesting that domain-specific knowledge acquired over time can contribute to "flowing, effortless performance, unhinged by analytical deliberations" (Flyvbjerg and Sampson 2001, p. 21; Salas, Rosen, and DiazGranados 2010). According to one study of police officers, there was a high level of consensus that failing to gather information from enough sources, not taking enough time overall to deal with the situation, and failing to consider enough alternatives, caused undesirable outcomes (Willis and Mastrofski 2017, p. 92).

Accounts of police competence also identify certain key skills, particularly verbal acuity, that minimize the need for physical exertion, or the assertion of formal authority by relying on other means such as questioning, persuading, negotiating, or threatening (Muir 1977; Fielding 1984, p. 570). From the perspective of police officers, the experienced officer only uses force as a last resort and then keeps it to the minimum necessary. In the words of Bittner (1990, pp. 191–192), good police officers, similar to experienced doctors, "must acquire the attitude of physicians who take pride in employing all available means to avoid surgery, and who, when surgery is unavoidable, take pride in the smallest possible incision." In a study of two relatively small police agencies (both less than 300 sworn), officers ranked knowledge of laws, rules, and regulations, people, places, and customs, negotiation, and verbal coercion (in descending order) as the top four skills or knowledge areas for promoting good police performance (Willis and Mastrofski 2017).

Finally, consistent with NDM (Klein 2015), the police craft emphasizes the importance of sorting through the information available in a given situation that can be complex and dynamic, processing it, and forming judgments about what is happening (Muir 1977). This decision-making process includes identifying relevant cues, finding ways to elicit information that is reliable, and then processing and evaluating the pattern of available information (Alpert and Rojek 2011). Sometimes this process can be crude and inaccurate, but ethnographers also describe the unusual aptitude of some exceptional officers for recognizing complex cues and analyzing situations carefully, and for their application of subtlety and skill to producing accurate judgments (Bittner 1967; Muir 1977; Kelling 1999). While it is common to identify two processes of cognition, System 1 (automatic, intuitive, and rapid) and System 2 (deliberative, abstract, and rule-based), in reality decisions are often a combination of both interacting in complex and parallel ways (Salas, Rosen, and DiazGranados 2010, p. 5).

2.6 Conclusion

Our examination of the several different systems for controlling discretion suggests that the views and experiences of patrol officers are rarely foremost in the minds of reformers. Even the dominant vision for policing as a skilled profession seems to find ways to constrain officer decision-making, rather than take account of officers' tremendous situational knowledge in making judgments about what to do. Moreover, an emphasis on developing generalizable scientific knowledge and broad rules or laws is rarely integrated with a deeper understanding of the context-dependent nature of patrol officer decision-making. For officers, unlike science, policing is a craft that cannot be "reducible to principle" (Bayley and Bittner 1984, p. 51). This is particularly true when it comes to making value judgments about what *ought* to be done in a particular encounter with the public. Abstract moral principles and general ethical guidelines are difficult to apply because questions about values are ultimately situated judgments and more easily addressed by examining specific individual cases (Thacher 2001). Nor do departments systematically solicit the views of community members on the nature and quality of individual police–community encounters.

In the next section, we describe a research study we conducted that sought to address some of these issues, in particular the potential for tapping into officers' direct experiences in order to derive standards for guiding and evaluating performance. We then use these insights as a basis for envisioning a more systematic craft learning model for improving police practice. A craft learning model can help contribute to police professionalism by revealing how demanding an activity patrol work can be, by attempting to develop criteria for distinguishing more from less skillful performance, and by having police officers accept greater responsibility for the many facets of their operational decision-making (Bayley and Bittner 1984, p. 56).

3 The Craft Learning Model

3.1 Deriving Craft-Based Standards

Standards for evaluating professional practice, although they often take the form of tacit knowledge, are central to being a profession. As Yanow and Tsoukas write (2009, p. 1347, internal citations omitted):

> [J]oining and participating in a practice necessarily involves attempting to achieve the standards of excellence operative in the practice at that time. Practices are organized human activities regulated by goals and standards. Unless one accepts the authority of both the standards of the practice into which one has entered and the judgments of acknowledged masters of that practice, one will never be accepted into that practice. Of course, standards of excellence change over time, and it is precisely such changes that practitioners often debate, especially when new members enter a practice. But for change to be intelligible, standards of excellence must be accorded ontological priority – they are a point of reference, albeit a contestable one, to guide behavior.

Even if a police action does not violate a policy, it might still fall far short of craft standards and principles. Rather than establishing minimal, rule-bound guidelines for performance, standards try to establish goals or ideals worth striving for, even if they can be hard to attain. This aspirational quality of standards is not easily captured by abstract and general rules. Moreover, since standards are being applied to the realities of actual practice, where situations can be ambiguous and unpredictable (Schön 1987), their application to police behavior requires flexibility in interpretation. Although standards can only act as guides to behavior, a standard and its related content help identify some of the key decision-making criteria in a given encounter and can provide a basis for distinguishing better from worse performance, or high-quality police work from work that is merely acceptable or unacceptable. In the same way that experts or master craftspeople can be identified by their virtuoso mental and physical skills, creativity, and desire to "do a job well for its own sake," craft standards can help distinguish superior performers from those who merely meet their minimal obligations (Sennet 2008, p. 9).

In their discussion of how standards work in the complex "realm of human affairs," Cohen and Feldberg (1991, pp. 39–40) observe:

> There is no standard handshake against which others can be measured. Neither is there one way to remove a drunk from a bar, calm a family dispute, or conduct an investigation. There are, of course, better and worse ways to do all these things. We still know that a frown is not just another way to smile, beating someone senseless is not another way to negotiate and threatening a person is not a way to make him or her feel relaxed. In short, even where precision is not possible, standards may be set. Those standards, however, must accommodate variation in the behavior that meets them while distinguishing it from behavior that does not meet them. At the edges, these standards will be open to interpretation and be, in effect, approximations of what we expect of human behavior.

A major road-block to improving street-level discretion is the view that "standards of excellence" cannot be "fully formulated in advance of the occasions of use," due to the extraordinarily varied situations police are required to handle (Bittner 1983, p. 3). Police practitioners push this claim furthest, by asserting that every situation is different and that their actions cannot be assessed fully or fairly by those not present at the actual scene. Any form of "Monday Morning Quarterbacking" by others (the tendency to criticize with the benefit of hindsight) is generally scorned and seen as intrusive, arbitrary, and unhelpful (Bayley and Bittner 1984). Not only is this perspective clearly "self-serving," it implies that the police craft is not amenable to in-depth analysis and formal learning (Bayley and Bittner 1984, p. 35).

However, even if specific types of street-level encounters are complex and uncertain, and do not lend themselves to strict and narrow evaluative criteria, this does not mean that it is impossible to identify broad operational goals worth pursuing, goals which could then provide a valuable basis for guiding and assessing decision-making (Bayley and Bittner 1984; Mastrofski 1996). In short, while it might be impossible to distill practice goals into simple rules that could be automatically applied to any given situation, this does not mean that performance dimensions cannot be identified ex ante for guiding discretion along more "principled routes" (Thacher 2016, p. 533). After all, any evaluation of police discretion (and a potential framework for reviewing and exploring its use) first requires the possibility of identifying defensible criteria for its assessment. Police scholars have long recognized the possibility of accessing police officers' intuitive knowledge based on their collective experiences to improve discretion, but few attempts have been made to advance this insight empirically, or to develop the logic, substance, and uses, of a craft-based learning model, especially in relation to its dominant rulemaking alternative.

In our research, we were curious whether patrol officers would identify similar performance standards, and so we examined this directly. Of course, we expected officers to think differently from one another about what comprises skilled police work in any specific situation (Goldstein 1979, p. 248). At the same time, we wondered if there was a sufficient level of consensus among patrol officers on what constituted high-quality performance to act as a useful tool. These standards could then act as a foundation for envisioning a craft model for improving police discretion in frontline decision-making's "swampy lowlands, where situations are confusing messes incapable of technical solution and usually involve problems of greatest human concern" (Schön 1983, p. 42). We also wanted to explore how this framework might help advance police officer understanding of the essential normative, or moral, elements of their decisions. These value judgments, powerfully shaped by situational contexts, tend to be implicit and rarely exposed to critical examination. And yet disagreements over normative considerations regarding what constitutes "doing the right thing" on the front lines of police work often lie at the heart of public controversies over police actions (Mastrofski 2018).

We describe this research, including our methodology and our results more fully elsewhere (Willis and Toronjo 2023)), so here we only sketch our approach and summarize the major findings. Briefly, we conducted in-depth interviews with thirty-eight patrol officers in one medium-sized police agency in the United States (around 300 sworn officers). As part of the interview, we asked respondents to react to the actions of two police officers in a video-taped incident involving a real-life dispute between two neighbors living in adjacent apartments. We selected this clip because it was an accurate depiction of the kind of fairly routine yet perplexing encounters that police confront. The immediate threat of violence appeared low, but the solution of how best to respond was not obvious (at least to us), especially given that one of the neighbors was uncooperative and rejected the officers' advice.

In the clip, one neighbor was upset and complained to the police that the neighbor living next to her had pounded on her door with a heavy metal weight leaving dents and had also threatened her. According to this complainant, the second neighbor was upset that she was slamming her door too loudly. When the officers spoke to the second neighbor, they were puzzled by the hostility of her reaction and tried to reason with her several times before eventually giving up. They ended the encounter by warning the second neighbor that if they had to return that night, she would be taken to the precinct. They then took the heavy metal weight and disposed of it down a trash chute.

We told the interviewees we were going to stop the video clip at a key decision point as the encounter was still evolving, and ask them to assess these officers' decisions and what they would have done differently. This was an attempt to replicate the evolving nature of the police decision-making environment, so that respondents would not have the benefit of knowing how the encounter ended in making their assessment. Using a combination of deductive and inductive analyses, we derived seven craft-based standards from officers' reactions: lawfulness, accountability, problem diagnosis, repair of harm, economy, safety and order, and fairness.

3.1.1 Lawfulness

As legal decision-makers, the public wants and expects police officers to comply with the law. Police compliance with the law is one of the essential elements of a democratic society (Skogan and Meares 2004, p. 66), and "the goal of ensuring lawfulness in police conduct finds expression in rules guarding individuals' rights to liberty and property, freedom from unreasonable intrusions, and fair and equal treatment" (Skogan and Frydl 2004, p. 5). Public perception that the police act lawfully is also an important source of police legitimacy (Mastrofski 1996, p. 220). Even if a police officer's behavior does not violate the law, it may undermine the spirit of the law and the values it seeks to uphold (such as autonomy, equality, and restraint). Research suggests that when police exercise their authority, they are most heavily influenced by legal factors associated with a situation, particularly the evidence of wrongdoing, the preferences of the complainant, and the seriousness of the suspected offense (Skogan and Frydl 2004, p. 115).

In the context of our clip, some key legal questions that arose were whether the officers did anything not permitted by law or omitted to do something. There was disagreement among our respondents about whether the neighbor dispute qualified as a criminal or civil matter, and whether there was sufficient evidence to make an arrest. Perspectives also differed on the seriousness of the offense, with some respondents considering the conflict as a possible harbinger of a serious assault or even homicide, while to others it was nothing more than a minor quarrel or falling-out between former friends. Some respondents were also troubled that the officers in the clip seemed to be actively discouraging the complainant from requesting an arrest, and that they took, and disposed of, the heavy metal weight without her permission (this was akin to theft according to some of our respondents). Interviewees' uncertainty about whether this was a civil or criminal matter, and about the evidentiary standards that applied, shows how police officers can struggle to interpret the law, even in those situations which might not appear on the surface to be legally complex (Heffernan and Lovely 1991; Gould and Mastrofski 2004).

3.1.2 Accountability

Another key dimension of police performance to emerge from our interviews was accountability. In addition to deterring undesirable conduct, a fundamental premise of US criminal law is that people are responsible for their actions toward others, especially when these may be harmful. The law is central to society's efforts "to build up each individual's sense of responsibility as a guide and a stimulus to the constructive development of his [sic] capacity for effectual and fruitful decision" (Hart 1958, p. 410). Members of the public will call the police when they feel wronged or treated unfairly. Central to the idea of being treated unfairly is the assignment of blame to the alleged wrongdoer, and the expectation that they will have to answer for their actions (Folger and Cropanzano 2001). One way for the police to do this is through arrest, but there are other more informal ways.

Only seven of our thirty-eight respondents said they would make an arrest, and so dealing with the situation informally was a much more popular choice than resorting to legal sanctions. This could take a variety of forms, including threatening or warning, persuading, and negotiating, and the officers in the clip tried all three during the course of the encounter. It is worth noting that the officers depicted appeared to be more eager to judge the second neighbor's vandalism as inappropriate and to admonish her accordingly than in learning about the circumstances that might have provoked, and potentially justified her response (at least in part). Similarly, some of our respondents adopted the same normative frame in focusing on judging and reprimanding the second neighbor as the blameworthy troublemaker (Stalans and Finn 1995). The second neighbor, in turn, refused to concede that her actions were unjustified, which seemed to frustrate both the officers in the clip and our respondents watching it. Other interviewees were more pragmatic; rather than focusing on chastising the second neighbor and assigning blame, they said they would consider ways to mitigate the situation by collaborating with both parties. In this regard, the more experienced officers among our respondents were less likely to favor an arrest. The most common response among our sample was to contact the building manager, or to mediate directly between the parties to find a solution, although there was disagreement over whether it would be best to counsel the two neighbors separately or together.

3.1.3 Problem Diagnosis

The effectiveness of an officer's response depends in no small measure on their ability to accurately diagnose the nature of the problem. Schön (1983, p. 19) calls this "problem setting," or the ability to take a tangled and confusing situation and frame it as something more manageable. In this respect, police are like doctors who work closely with a patient to find out where the actual problem lies (Mastrofski 1998, p. 174). This can be challenging for several reasons, including time and information constraints, and conflicting accounts of what happened. As an example, Muir (1977, p. 154) gives the scenario of a patrol officer observing a man slumped down in the driver's seat of a parked car outside a liquor store with a cap pulled over his eyes: Was he casing the joint to commit a robbery? Was he experiencing a heart attack? Was he drunk or high on drugs? Muir then describes the actions the officer took to better detect the man's purpose and to try and predict his actions in order to come up with an appropriate response.

In the case of the neighbor dispute, an accurate diagnosis would likely require responses to several questions: What prompted such a hostile reaction from the second neighbor to the door slamming? Had the police been called to this address before? Had the neighbors tried to resolve the door slamming on their own? Knowing which questions are most relevant to ask and how best to ask them can require considerable skill and understanding.

3.1.4 Repair of Harm

People call the police because they want an issue dealt with or resolved, and involving the police may be the last resort. Our interviewees were dissatisfied with the officers in the clip for doing too little to improve the immediate situation, with some complaining that they actually worsened it by making the second neighbor even more upset with their inquiries, by scolding her, and by persisting in giving her unsolicited advice. Even if a problem is not fully resolved, success can be measured by the capacity to change some key features of a problem, such as reducing tensions between the disputants, or following up with a building manager to discuss possible solutions. Respondents referred to this as needing to "do something more," or actions that went beyond just talking to the parties and leaving. Ideally, whatever the police do during an encounter would lead to long-term success rather than just short-term outcomes, but given limited time, resources, and instrumental knowledge on the best means to a given end, police officers cannot be expected to solve all of society's ills. Still, even if a situation cannot be resolved to everyone's satisfaction, people will be satisfied if they feel that an officer has responded conscientiously to their concerns and made a "good-faith" effort to achieve a favorable result (Mastrofski 1999, p. 2).

3.1.5 Economy

Officers in the clip spent about seven minutes handling the neighbor dispute, raising questions of whether this was an appropriate amount of time. After all, this is also time away from the police doing something else potentially more pressing, such as patrolling their beats, making traffic stops, or trying to solve other neighborhood problems. Our respondents may have been dissatisfied that the officers in the clip did not do more to mitigate or solve the dispute, but few provided a time estimate that could act as a guide for how much effort should be expended. Studies suggest that how long different officers spend on different police contacts (such as parties who are in conflict with one another) can vary dramatically (Mastrofski 1999, p. 6). Time can also be perceived as a measure of attentiveness – too little time and people may feel dismissed. Police organizations currently give little guidance on what level of economy, or "personal resource expenditure," is appropriate.

3.1.6 Safety and Order

While the risk of injury or death is higher in other occupations (e.g., construction, farming), police officers confront unpredictable situations, freighted with the potential for violence and physical injury to the officer, and to the civilians involved. Accordingly, officers assign high priority to maintaining safety and order on the scene. Also, no other goals can be achieved unless this is first accomplished. In a survey of two police agencies asking officers to rank top performance priorities, this standard was rated the most important (Willis and

Mastrofski 2017, p. 91). The neighbor dispute raised a number of safety concerns for our respondents, including the positioning of the officers in relation to the two apartments. Furthermore, while departments might generate automatic inquiries when any injury occurs, situations where injuries *could* have occurred are largely overlooked.

3.1.7 Fairness of the Process

The final standard to emerge from our interviews was "fairness," which is an essential normative feature of American law (Berrey, Hoffman, and Nielsen 2012, p. 2). Research suggests that even if the police cannot deliver the outcome people desire, members of the public care very much about how they are treated. Importantly, public perceptions of police fairness can contribute to police legitimacy (Tyler 2004). Police can convey fairness by giving all parties a voice, or the chance to tell their side of what happened, which can also contribute to feelings of group inclusion or being valued (Pennington and Farrell 2019). To demonstrate fairness, police should also listen attentively, show dignity and respect, and demonstrate that they are evenhanded and unbiased (Tyler 2004). People also care that an officer is concerned about their and/or the community's well-being. Many of our respondents felt that the officers in the clip generally behaved professionally but noted that there was room for improvement. Some, for example, noticed one of the officers briefly rolling his eyes while the second neighbor spoke, which could be interpreted as disparaging or dismissive.

These seven craft-based performance standards suggested to us that despite the "unavoidably complex" realities of police practice (Thacher 2019, p. 280), it *was* possible to identify criteria applicable to assessing performance in police–public encounters, in this case a neighbor dispute. We imagine a similar process to the one we describe here carried out by police agencies, but one designed around a small seminar setting with patrol officers. Ideally these officers would be recognized by their peers as skilled craftspeople. The focus of the discussions would be on providing plenty of opportunity for the sharing of different viewpoints, careful deliberation, and for building consensus (Mastrofski 1996). Standards would likely differ across different types of routine encounters distinguished by common features (e.g., disputes between strangers, or traffic stops), and departments could identify which encounters to prioritize for the development of their performance dimensions.

While the focus of our interview data was to explore empirically the feasibility of deriving craft-based performance standards, we go one step further by envisioning a model for how these standards might be integrated into a more systematic learning process for potentially improving practical decision-making and moral reasoning. One possibility is for first-line supervisors to apply these standards to BWC footage as part of regular performance reviews of their officers using a learning process of reflection-in-action.

3.2 Craft Standards, Supervisory Review, and Reflection-in-Action

First formulated by John Dewey (1933) and developed later by Donald Schön, reflection-in-action is part of an epistemology of practice whose point of departure is "the competence and artistry already embedded in skillful practice" (Schön 1987, p. xi). For Schön, the traditional focus of the professions on applying scientific theory and standardized knowledge to instrumental problem-solving (technical rationality) is of limited relevance to meeting the challenges of real-world decision-making (Schön 1983, p. 87). According to Schön, social science assumes problems can be abstracted from "messy problematic situations" and then solved, thereby overlooking the process whereby problems became defined. How problems are "set" or understood is not a technical problem, but one of interpretation whereby "we *name* the things to which we will attend and *frame* the context in which we will attend to them" (Schön 1983, p. 40, emphasis in original). Furthermore, routine responses may be inadequate for problems that are unique or unstable, and while scientific inquiry can help identify the best means to an agreed upon end (e.g., crime reduction), it cannot resolve conflicts between different ends (e.g., liberty versus crime control) (Schön 1983, p. 41; Thacher 2001). Schön suggests there is a hard, high ground of well-defined problems, where practitioners can rely more heavily on scientific theory and research, but it is in the swampy lowlands of actual practice where much of the organization's business gets done. Here pressing problems do not simply lend themselves to technical solutions (Schön 1983, p. 42).

Schön refers to this dichotomy as the dilemma between "rigor or relevance," and he argues for the greater development of professional knowledge "implicit in the artistic, intuitive processes which some practitioners [bring] to situations of uncertainty, instability, uniqueness, and value conflict" (Schön 1983, p. 49). Key to this artistry is the ability of some practitioners, especially experts, to "reflect in the midst of action without interrupting it," particularly when dealing with situations where a practitioner's more familiar problem-solving approach fails to deliver expected results (Schön 1983, p. 16; Schön 1987; p. 56). In these kinds of problematic situations, reflection-in-action, or "turning thought back on action" while a situation is occurring, can lead to more effective decision-making. By reflecting-in-action, a practitioner may change the initial framing of a problem, reconsider underlying assumptions, rethink a particular strategy, and conduct "on-the-spot" experiments (Schön 1983, pp. 62–63). This knowledge and understanding can then be applied effectively to similar situations in the future.

Because first-line supervisors are the "cornerstone" of police organizations and work closely with individual officers and instruct them on how they perform their craft (Muir 1977, p. 235; Engel and Worden 2003), they are appropriately situated to conduct such an interactive learning review. Unlike police work in the past, many police supervisors now have access to BWCs, which provide high-quality audio and video recordings. This footage can be used to help appraise how officers behave during encounters with the public, particularly those they experience as problematic (Nix, Todak, and Tregle 2020). It can capture a tremendous amount of detail, including variations in body language and tone of voice, and it can be played slowly and stopped to help officers recall what they were thinking in the actual context and moment of deciding. Thus, BWC footage can serve as part of a process of open-ended inquiry designed to help expose and interrogate the tacit decision-making processes essential to professional practice that so often remain unarticulated and unexamined (Yanow and Tsoukas 2009, p. 1342).

In describing reflection-in-action, Schön gives the example of an architectural design process, where a student engages with a studio master to design an elementary school (Schön 1987, ch. 3). Essential to this process is a discussion around the studio master's attempt to understand the student's actions in the context of doing them, the use of examples to demonstrate alternative responses, and the student's additional reflection on the implications of the studio master's insights. "Backtalk" or encouraging the student to recall and listen to the surprises the evolving situation presents and how these affect later actions is a key aspect of this conversation (Schön 1987, p. 31). If we imagine that the lead officer in the clip of the neighbor dispute was meeting with a supervisor to review his performance, we can try to envision what a similarly reflective process would look like in a policing context, and its potential benefits in helping officers come to a deeper appreciation of a given situation.

To begin, the use of established standards could provide a framework for the review by helping narrow the potentially dizzying array of choices to some of the most relevant for judging the quality of decision-making. This helps make any evaluation less overwhelming and more coherent. A driving question is how well did the officer take these standards into account? Take problem identification, for example. In the clip, the second neighbor's obstinacy in refusing to admit she had done anything wrong flummoxed the officers and they never really recovered. Each time the lead officer insisted she had behaved wrongly toward her neighbor, she responded that the first neighbor was in the wrong for slamming her door. In her mind, her retaliation was justified by her neighbor's wrongful behavior. By relying primarily on a normative framework for assigning blame, the officers' attempts at moral persuasion quickly resulted in a stalemate – an end that one familiar with motivational interviewing (MI) might have predicted. Known as "righting reflex" within the practice of MI, the belief that you can easily *persuade* a person to do the right thing runs counter to what science tells us about the human brain and motivation processes (Miller & Rollnick 2012).

Having an officer talk through the problem they thought they were facing and identify some of the limits to their usual response is an obvious opportunity for backtalk and reflection. A sergeant could use open-ended questions and probes to help an officer reflect on the actions that led to this roadblock, as the situation was occurring. One approach aimed at helping learners use experiences to improve their practice is David Kolb's experiential learning theory. This process would help the officer reflect on their experience in a way meant to help induce them to experiment with a different approach in the future (Kolb 2014). Discussions rooted in experiential learning theory may wind their way through four processes: the concrete activity, reflective observation, abstract conceptualization, and planning active experimentation (though presented as such in the theory, real conversations need not neatly walk through the various stages in a tidy cycle). As an illustration, the sergeant might ask the officer to reflect on their experience, including their emotions and thoughts during the encounter. They might be encouraged to think about their previous experience, and how the officer considered this encounter different or similar to others. During the conversation, the sergeant may have the officer connect the citizen's response to an abstract idea such as "motivation" and how motivation works (consider our officers in the clip and their use of moral persuasion). This may lead to an opportunity where both sergeant and officer probe their assumptions about what they know of this abstract concept. It might be an opportunity for both parties to ask themselves those all-important self-appraising questions such as, "What do we know about this?" "How do we know it?" "How might we be wrong?" And "How could we be sure?"

A sergeant speaking with one of the two officers from the clip might ask how the officer's assumption that this was a minor dispute may have contributed to the second neighbor feeling like her interests or concerns were being too readily overlooked. What might help explain why the second neighbor was so resistant to their advice? Perhaps in "setting" this problem as a minor disturbance, the officer closed themselves off from taking more interest in identifying and understanding the problem's causes and effects, including some complicating factors that might have been at play. One of the neighbors mentioned that they used to be good friends. How might knowing more about the nature of the neighbors' past relationship change this officer's characterization of the problem? What might have caused them to overlook this factor? Maybe they simply did not hear the neighbor's comment about them once being friends. How might discovering more about the nature of door slamming have changed the characterization of the problem? How often was the door slamming occurring and what time of the day? Was it waking the second neighbor up at night and affecting her job performance, or making her so tired that she could not function ably? It can be easy to dismiss noise complaints as minor irritants, but they are some of the commonest problems brought to the police, and

> while some of those complaining may be petty or unreasonable, many are seriously aggrieved and justified in their appeal for relief: Sleep is lost, schedules are disrupted, mental and emotional problems are aggravated. Apartments become uninhabitable. The elderly woman living alone, whose life has been made miserable by inconsiderate neighbors, is not easily convinced that the daily intrusion into her life of their noise is any less serious than other forms of intrusion. For this person, and for many like her, improved policing would mean a more effective response to the problem of the noise created by her neighbors (Goldstein 1979, p. 247).

To help the officer consider future actions, some of the supervisor's queries could be framed as "what might happen" questions: What might happen if next time they do more to learn about the nature of the problem and its seriousness *before* assigning blame? What might happen if they try to help the next agitated person voice their own reasons for wanting to resolve the dispute? To aid this reflective process, it may be helpful if departments developed the content of each standard more fully. This could help give supervisors and their officers additional guidance on how their performance "measured up." For example, the standard of problem identification could be described as:

> Using available resources, including the parties involved, to conduct a broad and thoughtful inquiry into the specific nature of the problem. The purpose of the inquiry is to develop a deeper understanding of the problem by defining the problem accurately (including its frequency and how long it's been occurring), by defining possible underlying causes through open-ended questions and follow-up probes, and by assessing carefully the seriousness of its effects.

With this standard as a guide, supervisors could identify more specific areas for improvement and help officers achieve higher levels of performance. Importantly, in helping officers reflect, supervisors might bring their own repertoire of experiences to bear. These could range across similar disputes and include solutions a supervisor might have tried in relation to features similar to this particular dispute.

Last, some standards might lend themselves to a more precise form of performance assessment, but to a useful degree, fairness could be assessed by a sergeant's qualitative evaluation of an officer's actions in relation to each of the four elements of procedural justice (voice, dignity and respect, neutrality, and trustworthy motives). Again, the purpose would be to have the officer reflect actively on what they did to demonstrate fairness and anticipate changes they may make in the future and this process of deliberation could be repeated for the other standards. Was there room for improvement in terms of how the officer demonstrated fairness? Did the officer hold the second neighbor sufficiently accountable for her actions?

3.3 Potential Benefits of Reflection-in-Action

The reliance on thoughtfully reflective deliberation and learning in the context of actual incidents as they evolve helps distinguish craft-based learning reviews from an administrative rulemaking model. One potential benefit is the opportunity to identify whether an officer's goals are consistent with those of the agency, and whether their actions are consistent with existing policies and procedures. The latter could be a basis for the officer to revise their goals, or for the agency to establish clearer expectations for what its officers should be trying to accomplish. Using this case as an example, a department might suggest its officers expend more time and effort to repair the harm that caused the vandalism of the neighbor's door than the officers depicted.

This review of an officer's choices goes well beyond prescriptive or "rule-governed" inquiry (Schön 1987, p. 34), whether informed by bureaucratic or scientific knowledge. By encouraging officers to think about what they were thinking and trying to accomplish, particularly in the context of the challenges they were experiencing as they were occurring, reflection-in-action would not be

> the leisurely, systematic, ex-post-facto rehearsing and critiquing of the he-saids-she-saids of an interaction (the kind of "Monday-morning quarterbacking" of "And then I did this because he said that, so I did this other thing . . .") that would suggest a stepping-back-and-engaging-the-question characteristic of detached reflection. Instead, we see in it the "online," "real-time," in-the-midst-of-it-all seemingly "split second" judgments that lead the practitioner in different directions from the established, routine practice. (Yanow and Tsoukas 2009, p. 1355)

The police culture places high value on the skill of talking (Willis and Mastrofski 2017), and the use and development of verbal facility is integral to the overall quality of the reflective process. Muir's police professionals were skilled talkers and were able to use words to capture fine-grained details and make subtle distinctions about people, behavior, and situations, particularly in terms of assessing measures of degree (i.e., the difference between being drunk, tipsy, or just drinking, or conduct which was "mousy," "overbearing," and "aggressive") (Muir 1977, p. 164). Should the second neighbor be labeled as petty, uncooperative, and defensive, or was she someone who was strong-willed, but who felt deeply wronged that no one seemed to be taking her grievance seriously? Based on his observations, Muir concluded that "far from being mere semantic quibbles, these characterizations of nuance sharpened a policeman's discriminatory powers no end" (Muir 1977, p. 164). Schön (1987, p. 61) makes a similar argument, noting how good architectural designers are able to attend to features of a situation by using words to detect "multiple references, distinguish particular meanings in context, and use multiple references as an aid to vision across design domains." Supervisors could help demonstrate the importance of variation in language in their framing of the problem and its participants, and the potential implications of how these are articulated for different decisions. We can also imagine a supervisor asking an officer to consider to what extent *how* they worded their specific questions helped solicit useful information, or whether they needed to be altered to better capture the realities and subtleties of the dispute.

Assessments of what constitutes more or less desirable exercises of police authority can obviously be complicated and controversial, particularly when law, policy, and science offer limited guidance. How then would a supervisor help an officer understand whether their performance was substandard, merely adequate, high quality, or truly exemplary? In some cases, this will be easy, such as when an officer clearly violated policy, or well-established norms of professional conduct. In more complex situations, as David Thacher (2020, p. 762) suggests, there is no simple answer to this question, as a craft model is highly contextual and "fundamentally open-ended." It is worth noting that this challenge is not unique to policing. Professionals in other fields, such as medicine and law, may struggle to reach a "firm and uncontroversial evaluation of a particular decision" (Thacher 2020, p. 762). This is also true of science, where the underlying assumption is that "nothing is every completely settled, that all knowledge is just probable knowledge" (Gawande 2016). From the perspective of the craft learning model, this observation opens up rather than closes down the dialogue during the review process. A benefit of standards is that they are grounded in the unsettled reality of street-level performance and not merely the aspirations of police administrators (Thacher 2008). They acknowledge honestly that patrol officers' choices must be seen according to the inherent situational complexity that they actually confront, "not as we wish it be" (Brown 1981, p. xii). With relevance and reality in mind, the key purpose of supervisory review is to help officers reflect actively on their choices, try to articulate how they tried to meet or exceed performance standards, how and why they might have fallen short, and consider areas for improvement.

Other concerns revolve around police officer bias and police norms rooted in the existing police culture that might contribute to troubling police practices, such as favoring wealthy over poor suspects, or treating civilians differently due to their race or gender (Lum 2009). Identifying standards for supervisory review is clearly not sufficient for preventing questionable or morally indefensible decision-making (Thacher 2016). To mitigate these concerns, departments could involve community members in a similar but separate approach for examining BWC footage. The purpose would be to solicit input on officer performance (Waddington et al. 2015). In this respect, the craft learning model overlaps with the democratic dimensions of the administrative rulemaking model, which requires that police agencies solicit civilian feedback on police policies (Davis 1975). In addition to the principles of transparency and community participation, a virtue of this approach is that policies (and the police practices they are intended to govern) will be refined "because those policies that cannot withstand public scrutiny will be minimized or eliminated" (Klockars 1985, p. 108). Similarly, community members' insights on officer performance could be part of the process for formulating standards and identifying responses that are consistent with community values and expectations. While examples of troubling applications of the police craft will undoubtedly remain, creating a system for thoughtfully reviewing and critiquing officer performance to help increase transparency, solicit community input, foster discussion, and improve external accountability would be a considerable step forward in monitoring and managing everyday uses of police authority (Mastrofski 1996).

Although it cannot offer a definitive guide to action, reflection-in-action structured around performance standard makes officers less vulnerable to arbitrary ex post facto assessments of their actions (Mastrofski 1996, p. 223). In fact, the participatory and respectful review process of the craft learning model advances the same kind of "humanistic democratic values" around authority relations that patrol officers are encouraged to use in their interactions with civilians (Angell 1971, p. 187). Evidence suggests that when police officers feel they are being treated fairly and justly within their own agencies, they are more likely to consider the organization's rules as legitimate and less likely to engage in misconduct (Tyler, Callahan, and Frost 2007).

Moreover, observations and conversations around specific standards can help with identifying gaps in an officer's knowledge and skills that might require additional training. For example, when it came to lawfulness in our neighbor dispute, there was disagreement among respondents about whether and how this standard applied in this specific context. This is a valuable insight, as the law is an important source of self-guidance for patrol officers and a means for expanding or narrowing the range of decision-making options to consider. Recognizing the range of legal options available to an officer admits the possibility of a more artful response. Additionally, knowing more clearly what the law does not permit can help set limits on a police officer's sense of responsibility, giving them "sanctuary from public blame and self-criticism" (Muir 1977, p. 259). Giving patrol officers' ownership in defining and developing performance criteria, rather than imposing regulations from above, may also increase acceptance of the new model of reviewing and guiding discretion.

Learning about officers' attempts and their decision-making architecture could also lead to innovation and broader organizational learning, as some practitioners adapt to surprise by considering creative solutions. Patrol officers might share their insights with one another informally, but departments have few structures in place to tap the creative possibilities of actual police practice (Thacher 2008). Rather than adhering to the more standardized response of talking to both parties and issuing a warning, one of our interviewees suggested padding the frame of the neighbor's door with rubber to deaden the noise. Once shared, these kinds of creative insights could become part of other officers' knowledge base when seeking to repair harm in future incidents that share similar features as the neighbor dispute (Schön 1987).

This kind of performance review could also help supervisors identify the evidence-based research that was particularly relevant to a specific type of encounter, and what this research suggests are some of the most promising approaches for managing some of the most challenging aspects of complex social interactions involving conflict, including de-escalation tactics and procedural justice (Wolfe et al. 2020). In turn, scientific knowledge about the likely outcomes of their decisions could help officers make more informed decisions, such as whether separating disputants is more effective at resolving interpersonal conflicts than talking to them together.

Finally, reflection-in-action helps identify important normative concerns. One of the most obvious regarding our neighbor dispute was the legality and advisability of making an arrest. Respondents' differing opinions on the appropriateness of this approach helps raise a central concern in policing. In a democracy which seeks to minimize government intrusions on individual liberty, police officers must strive to be as judicious as possible when deciding to take a person into custody (Harmon 2016). Any consideration of the appropriateness of an arrest must go beyond simply assessing the lawfulness of an arrest. It must include its substantial "physical, financial, psychological, or social" costs, whether these are "to suspects, families, officers, or communities" (Harmon 2016, p. 320). Officers must also weigh other values relevant to justifying an arrest decision, such as proportionality in matching their response to the seriousness of the second neighbor's conduct. Proportionality is fundamental to notions of fairness. In this case, did the suspect deserve to be arrested for the harms she caused in damaging the complainant's door and making threats, and how much should this assessment of her blameworthiness depend on a prior record of similar outbursts? We return to this issue in the next section when we discuss practical rationality as a framework for ethical decision-making.

While researchers may have no superior claim to moral expertise than a practitioner, a benefit of being a stranger to the police craft is the "distance and nearness, indifference and involvement" this role affords (Simmel 1908/1950). On account of this outsider's perspective, a researcher can help identify police officers' implicit value judgments that may have become taken for granted over time, so that officers can be re-sensitized to their relevance. They can also play a role in their meaningful critique (Thacher 2001). As Bayley and Bittner (1984, p. 55) have argued, "Experience may teach, but it rigidifies." A training program that has Baltimore police officers read James Baldwin, John Steinbeck, and Plato captures some of the elements of this approach. Its aim is to have officers reflect on the human condition and the meaning of complex values, such as respect (Dagan 2017).

In sum, while there might not be unanimous consensus on whether or not to arrest, a craft learning model might be able to contribute to more principled choices. It would do so by helping officers engage more fully with their own moral intuitions (which are often made quickly and with little reflection) (Haidt 2001), and by helping them refine their reasons for their value judgements (or even revise the judgements themselves). Although police agencies generally create abstract occupational or professional codes of expected conduct (Kleinig 2005), officers need guidance and experience applying these to the features of a specific situation in order to help them develop their moral reasoning.

3.4 Conclusion

In this section, we outlined the elements of a craft learning model, including how standards might be derived and applied through a process of reflection-in-action. This is built on the key assumption that patrol officer decision-making is context dependent, and that professional knowledge gained through experience is an important source of learning and guidance. In the next section, we consider four main challenges to this model that we anticipate based largely on our own knowledge and research on the police: (1) misalignment with police culture, (2) the limited role of first-line supervisors, (3) the current lack of community participation in guiding decision-making on the front lines, and (4) the problem of conflicting values. We also make some suggestions for how these challenges might be mitigated or overcome.

4 Challenges to a Craft-Based Learning Model

4.1 Misalignment with the Traditional Police Culture – Need for Leadership

The values, norms, and beliefs that constitute police officers' shared outlooks toward each other, their jobs, and the agencies for which they work develop in response to pressures in their internal organizational and external environments. As officers are drilled to understand in the academy (Blumberg et al. 2019), dealing with crime problems and strangers is laden with uncertainty, and street encounters carry the risk of disorder and violence. The department's paramilitary hierarchy can also present a threat to police officers, with its emphasis on punishment and accountability. Consequently, police officers are highly sensitive to safety issues and develop a sense of mutual dependence to protect themselves from management oversight and control (Loftus 2010). Police solidarity (including the 'blue wall of silence') also helps buffer officers from the complaints and criticisms of civilians (Paoline 2003) who are seen as quick to judge, untrustworthy, and unable to appreciate the centrality of coercion to the police role. Autonomy is also a central theme of the police culture, whereby officers place high value on their ability to exercise independent judgment over when and how they use their authority (Paoline 2003).

Scholars have long observed that the traditional police culture can undermine reform efforts and influence how officers think about and respond to the public (Cordner 2017). We anticipate that officers' perspectives on their role as crime fighters and the uncertainty and unpredictability of police work, their strong sense of solidarity, and their desire for autonomy will present significant challenges to the craft learning model (we discuss the challenge patrol officer perceptions of administrative oversight and accountability present in the following section on supervision).

While some officers might embrace efforts to improve performance around less serious crime and disorder problems, those who regard themselves primarily as crime fighters are less likely to do so. Steve Herbert (1998, 356) describes "hardchargers" as those officers who thrive on danger and the adrenalin rush of chasing and capturing those suspected of committing serious crimes: "In short, hardchargers are police warriors and exemplify such typically masculine characteristics as courage and strength." An ideology of police work based on chases, arrests, and gang suspects does not comport well with a learning model centered on more mundane police encounters, and its emphasis on in-depth and reflective decision-making (Brown 1981). Similarly, police officers' overriding preoccupation with safety (no matter how remote a threat a specific encounter presents) and their proclivity toward treating the public with suspicion could easily undermine a less cynical and less judgmental policing approach. Some evidence suggests that when departments are reviewing BWC performance footage, they are much more likely to focus attention on officer and public safety than a broader set of performance dimensions (Koen and Mathna 2019; Koen, Newell, and Roberts 2021; Willis 2022).

The craft learning model relies on a spirit of open inquiry and willingness to accept critical feedback, but the importance the police culture places on patrol officers' loyalty to one another, and on mutual respect, would likely subvert interest in systematic critiques of individual officer's performance. Research suggests that officers attending regular Compstat meetings for assessing middle mangers' performance were generally reluctant to share their insights lest their comments be interpreted as overly critical (Willis, Mastrofski, and Weisburd 2007). Moreover, a recent study on BWCs showed that officers seldom volunteered to share their footage with others to avoid being subject to faultfinding, and possibly unfair or disrespectful judgments from their peers. When officers were asked about any potential concerns around the use of BWC footage for performance reviews, they frequently mentioned the challenge of "feeling uncomfortable about having their actions closely scrutinized by other officers and being targeted for unfair criticism. For example, one patrol officer said that police officers had "Type A personalities, and don't like being criticized, while another said the primary obstacle was the culture of the agency, which did not encourage critical feedback" (Willis 2022, p. 14).

Concern or respect for officer autonomy may cause police agencies to be reluctant to engage in a process that subjects individual decision-making to more frequent and closer examination. According to Michael Brown (1981, p. 85):

> The values of the police culture derive from the hazards of police work and seek to minimize these hazards and protect group members. As long as a patrolman accepts these norms and meets his mutual obligations to the

group, he is free to use his powers of discretion as he sees fit. The same beliefs that lead policemen to attempt to minimize external control over their actions, operate within police departments to minimize second-guessing and allow each officer to exercise his independent judgment in each situation. Loyalty and individualism are thus opposite sides of the same coin: the police culture demands loyalty but grants autonomy.

Mitigating or overcoming these features of the police culture will undoubtedly require strong leadership, a key feature of organizational change too easily overlooked (Zimring 2017; Worden and Dole 2019, p. 50; Perry, Weisburd, and Hasisi 2023). Police administrators will need to articulate the values for their organizations that evince a clear commitment to high-quality police performance, organizational learning, and continuous improvement (Wasserman and Moore 1988). In his vision for problem-oriented policing, Herman Goldstein (1990, p. 153) argued that leaders "cannot be neutral," but "they must stand for something. They must have a set of values—a commitment, goals, and governing principles." In turn, this vision must be supported with broader structural changes, such as training. In addition, the implementation of a craft learning model would be strengthened, if it became part of a rewards system that included promotion. In their studies on police corruption and misconduct, Klockars and colleagues (2005) describe how police leadership can contribute to an organizational culture of integrity. In the same way, top administrators could help build a culture of craft by recognizing the value of professional knowledge and the examination of individual encounters to improve discretion. Fortunately, the craft learning model's involvement of patrol officers in the creation of standards might increase the likelihood of success, given that widespread participation in change processes can lower internal resistance (Loftus 2022, pp. 48–49)

4.2 Limited Role of First-Line Supervisors – Need for Coaching

The craft learning model also calls for the development of different leadership dimensions to first-line supervision. The emphasis on sergeants offering direction and practical guidance through coaching and reflection would be a major change from the kind of command-and-control supervisory model that has dominated policing and been under attack over the last forty years (Weisburd et al. 2003). Herman Goldstein suggests this traditional facet of police organizational management is resistant to change because the emphasis on simple and accessible measures of success (e.g., arrests and citations) and on the rank hierarchy makes it much easier for sergeants to routinely assess officer performance based on traditional indicators and to rely on their authority to influence behavior rather than using their "intellect and interpersonal skills" (Goldstein 1990, p. 157).

Moreover, the failures of past reform efforts are due at least in part to the lack of buy-in from patrol supervisors (Walker 1993).

Sergeants are probably the most important organizational members in a patrol officer's professional life, and traditionally are part of a police organization's internal control system, acting as both a "boss" and a "critical audience" for patrol officer performance (Van Maanen 1983, p. 279). They also tend to be more experienced officers and thus often have more practical knowledge to share than newer officers. However, how supervisors give direction to their officers and hold them accountable is complicated by the high degree of "mutual dependence and reciprocity" that governs these supervisor–subordinate relationships, and by the varied mechanisms that supervisors use to try to influence their officers' behaviors (Van Maanen 1983, p. 280). Generally, a sergeant's role has been to monitor their officers' activities and enforce departmental rules and regulations (Manning 1997). All of this occurs in a supervisory context based on the exchange of favors through a system of contingent rewards and punishment (Van Maanen 1983). Some supervisors may enforce bureaucratic rules, while others may broker compliance by protecting their officers from department discipline in return for their being productive and staying out of trouble (Engel and Worden 2003). Not only does this give rise to different styles of supervisory practice that might not be suited to a craft learning model, but also supervisors are often reluctant to intervene in an officer's operational decision-making. Van Maanen (1983, p. 288) describes how sergeants must walk a "thin line" in showing up on calls in order to ensure that they do not violate their officers' strong sense of independence: "Whatever self-initiated activities they undertake in the process of displaying their capacity to monitor must be carefully constrained lest those supervised come to feel that they are being supervised and spied on."

In such a risk-averse environment, sergeants' reticence to take on a more regular hands-on role in the development of their officers' practical knowledge and skills, and their capacity for good judgment, is revealed in many departments' BWC policies. A content examination of BWC policies submitted by 304 agencies that received federal BWC awards between FY 2015 and FY 2018 revealed that compared to using BWC footage for administrative reviews (e.g., use of force, officer injury), or in response to civilian complaints, reviewing footage as part of a broader assessment of patrol officer performance was more "contentious" (White and Malm 2020, p. 68). Indeed, some departments specifically *exclude* using footage for this purpose in case it undermines morale or encourages "fishing" expeditions that "jam" officers up for minor violations of department policy (Snyder, Crow, and Smylka 2019). In a case study of some of the challenges of implementing BWCs, one department's BWC policy specifically forbade sergeants from using cameras as part of a more systematic performance review process, stating: "Supervisors may access and review BWC video of officers directly under their command, however, this should not be done on a routine basis to simply review employee performance. Any such review is permitted as follow-up to a complaint investigation or any other on-going training or performance related issue."

Sergeants and officers supported this provision since cameras were strongly associated with the identification of policy violations as part of an administrative investigation, rather than a tool for advancing learning about the police craft (Willis 2022).

A craft learning model would require a change to this kind of operational philosophy rooted in bureaucratic accountability. Supervisors would be expected to develop their subordinates to higher levels of "ability and potential" (Bass and Avolio 1994, p. 2) and place greater emphasis on encouraging officers to analyze their own decision-making critically and to think creatively. Other police scholars have suggested the importance of supervisors behaving as coaches, who rely less on their formal authority and more on their experience as skilled professionals. Muir (1977), for example, suggested the potential influence of this dimension of police supervision on officer behavior, and some evidence suggests that supervisors who lead by example can have a significant effect on officer decision-making (Engel 2002, p. 6).

The concept of a coach can be "slippery," but coaches mainly observe, judge, and guide as an extra set of "ears and eyes" for someone's work (Feldman and Lankau 2005; Gawande 2011). Atul Gawande, the surgeon and author, describes how he asked a more experienced colleague to watch him at work to improve his effectiveness in the operating theater, after his surgical performance had plateaued. In this role as coach, Gawande's colleague asked him questions about critical components of his performance, picking out fine-grained details about his positioning in the operating theater, and elements of his craft that he seemed to miss, such as a drop in the patient's blood pressure. According to Gawande, he was given more to consider after a twenty-minute discussion with his coach following a particular thyroidectomy than in the past five years.

The job of a coach is to empower employees while also to facilitate learning. In their study of coaching behaviors in learning organizations, Ellinger and Bostrum (1999, p. 758) identify several key elements of good coaching. Rather than directing, controlling, and prescribing behavior, coaches encourage employees to take more responsibility and accountability for their decisions, and they use questions to help them think through an issue, including the consequences of their actions. Good coaches also try to facilitate learning through collaboration and discovery, and by acting as a guide to decision-making. Undoubtedly, coaching is challenging, and some police supervisors will lack the necessary skills and attributes. Ideally, police supervisors recognized as master craftsmen by their peers would take on this role, but there is no guarantee that they could coach others.

Training police supervisors to be better coaches could help overcome some of these barriers, and there are models in other areas of criminal justice supervision that could prove to be instructive. For example, there are training programs in corrections designed to help develop probation supervisors' professional skills via experiential learning and continuous coaching (Bonta and Andrews 2016; Toronjo 2019, 2020). In policing, a major reform effort to create a new "quality policing" model in Madison, Wisconsin, suggests it is possible to incorporate coaching as an element for improving police services (Couper and Lobitz 1991). There is also evidence that coaching can be an effective tool for improving employee performance in medicine (Ervin 2005), child welfare (Barbee et al. 2011), psychology (D. Milne 2009), teaching (Joyce & Showers 2002), and other human service fields (Feldman and Lankau 2005, p. 836). For example, a study examining the use of videos for postoperative reviews, involving typical or challenging surgical events, concluded that they could facilitate coaching sessions and could help improve patient outcomes (Ibrahim, Varban, and Dimick 2016).

4.3 Lack of Community Participation – Need for Engagement

As we have discussed, advocates of the administrative rulemaking model in the 1970s argued that community input could help improve police policy by exposing it to greater public scrutiny and assessment. More recently, the President's Taskforce on Twenty-First Century Policing (2015, p. 19) reaffirmed the importance of sharing policies externally, so that they might be "reflective of community values and not lead to disparate impacts on various segments of the community."

Similarly, a craft learning model includes efforts to strengthen democratic policing by increasing accountability between the police and the public, and by soliciting feedback from community members to help guide police decision-making. Bittner (1983, pp. 7–8) made a similar argument when examining "workmanship" (i.e., craft) as a mechanism of police organization and control, since ultimately police officers should be acting on the community's behalf:

> It is quite clear that the criteria of workmanship and procedures for examining it must be developed from within policing. The purely technical aspects of workmanship in policing can only acquire formulation and development

from the practitioners of the craft themselves. But, as is well known, policing cannot be reduced to the mere exercise of a technical craft; it is, in the first place, a public trust. Therefore, the audit of workmanship must ultimately be public. The central point here is that the police are publicly accountable not merely to the extent of not being wrong but, beyond that, for being right. Naturally, the public is entitled to assurances that officers will not transgress any explicit regulations on doing their work, but it is also entitled to assurances that they will act with the degree of prudence, foresight, and technical acumen that distinguishes them from lay persons.

Giving community members the opportunity to view and comment on BWC footage of an officer's performance is part of the process for distinguishing better from worse policing, and for identifying police responses consistent with community values and expectations. Police departments could do much more to learn community members' views on the relevant priorities in a specific type of encounter and the appropriate practices for trying to accomplish them. Department leadership could take this broader feedback and even decide to add or refine its existing craft standards, and how they are applied. Of course, this approach raises difficult issues around the kind of forum best suited to advancing these goals, the nature of community representation and influence, and potential risks to the police department.

According to some, it is ordinary people and not the police who are primarily responsible for the current crisis around poor police performance. This is due to the public's failure to fulfill its obligation to participate directly in the formulation of rules for guiding police (Friedman 2017). Others are more skeptical that increased public involvement in policymaking will cure policing. After all, public participation at the local government level is often fairly low and any significant increases are unlikely to be achievable (Worden and Dole 2019, p. 48). Even in Chicago, which made one of the most comprehensive and ardent attempts to implement community policing by assigning teams of officers to 279 different beats, it was "surprisingly difficult" to engage community members in police matters (Skogan and Roth 2004, p. xxvii). Despite the creation of the city-wide Chicago Alternative Policing Strategy (CAPS), less than 1 percent of the adult population attended these meetings. Some of this reluctance can likely be attributed to Chicago's long and troubled history with some of its most disadvantaged communities, which has recently been revealed more fully. The city's own Police Accountability Task Force (formed in the wake of the US Department of Justice's consent decree following the police department's murder (and subsequent cover up) of teenager Laquan McDonald in 2015) found a "long, sad history of death, false imprisonment, physical and verbal abuse and general discontent about police actions in neighborhoods of color" (Force P.A.T. 2016, p. 7).

Given levels of community apathy and possibly fear toward local government and policing, it would be easy for a police chief to simply select a few motivated community stakeholders to participate in the craft learning model, especially those who were most supportive of the department and its leadership. This, of course, would give a highly selective and distorted view of what the community desires from its police (Worden and Dole 2019). The same problem can hinder community policing initiatives, as certain groups are more likely to participate in police–community meetings than others (Mastrofski 1988). In Chicago, for example, there was "a strong middle-class bias in participation" in neighborhood beat meetings, and the community policing program struggled to integrate "marginalized groups with fewer mechanisms for voicing their concerns" (Skogan and Roth 2004, p. xxviii). There was even evidence of homeowner block groups being used as part of the CAPS program to encourage more conservative elements of the community to work with the police (Vanecko 2020). Thus, police leaders should intentionally solicit diverse perspectives to comment on police officer performance, including from those who come from disadvantaged neighborhoods, lack political influence, and are more likely to experience the sharp spur of police power (Gau and Brunson 2010). It might also well be worth considering involving other professionals, such as domestic violence advocates, street outreach workers, mental health specialists, or judges, who could provide helpful insights that might not have occurred to the police and that could contribute to additional learning about discretionary responses (Mastrofski 1996).

Unlike more serious criminal offenses, there is likely to be less community consensus about how the police should respond to more ambiguous situations, particularly those that involve some level of conflict or disorder. Deliberately inviting diverse viewpoints makes it even less likely that groups will agree about the most appropriate or desirable police response: "If police solicit such participation from diverse, alienated, even hostile segments of the community, they will undoubtedly find it more difficult to elicit and perceive a *single* expression of the community will. Discussions and debates will sometimes be chaotic, seemingly trivial, and endless" (Greene and Mastrofski 1993, p. 91).

In some ways, the craft learning model invites conflict. Nonetheless, the goal would not be consensus, but giving people an opportunity to voice reactions to what they see and hear in a BWC video clip. In a study exploring the perceptions and interpretations of police actions captured on video (including a traffic stop) by thirty-four diverse focus groups, the researchers observed conflicting and contradictory evaluations from the public about the behavior of the police (Waddington et al. 2015). Nonetheless, they concluded (Waddington et al. 2015, p. 233) that this process was vital for the professional education of police officers; it could help them "explicitly acknowledge and confront both the uncertainty that suffuses their working environment and also the controversy that almost inevitably surrounds it." Within the specific context of the craft learning model, community feedback could help police leaders better understand the public's concerns and desires around police performance in specific encounters with the police, and their views on the methods police use to handle certain problems. For example, in the case of the neighbor dispute, how satisfactory was the solution offered by the two officers in the clip, and to what degree would community members support an arrest under these conditions?

It is possible that members of the public would be motivated to engage directly in evaluations of the police craft, given the potential of their participation to influence how policing is done. To sustain interest, police executives would need to demonstrate a willingness to take this feedback seriously, and not simply to use the community for their own ends (Cheng 2022). Acting disingenuously would likely undermine community participation and increase criticism of the police (Mastrofski and Greene 1993, p. 93). On the other hand, publicly acknowledging the highly discretionary nature of patrol officer decision-making is a risky proposition for police departments. It could make policing more difficult by undermining the police "image of impartiality and objectivity" and by exposing officers to the challenges of civilians who feel that they are being treated unequally or unfairly compared to others (Klockars 1985, p. 107). At the same time, ignoring the fact that discretion lies at the core of police work perpetuates the unsatisfactory status quo, and it does little to recognize the degree of professionalism that high-quality decision-making in complex situations demands.

4.4 Conflicting Values – Need for Practical Wisdom

The plurality of fundamental values officers inevitably face in their encounters with civilians means they have to make choices about the proper combination of these values from an ethical and practical standpoint. Selecting between alternatives is obviously not unique to policing, as people also struggle, for example, to balance their autonomy with the desire for community. The justifications we use in making our decisions can be based on our actions having inherent value, or because they are instrumental in helping us achieve something else that has value (Mastrofski 2004). In our neighbor dispute, we have identified several relevant values, which can complicate an officer's decision-making calculus, especially when they conflict. How are such tensions to be reconciled? Should liberty trump safety, or vice versa? How much of a commitment to examining the nature of a problem should be sacrificed for efficiency?

At the heart of such value conflict is the idea that fundamental values are incommensurable with one another, meaning they "share no common measure and are not subject to any superior value" (Crowder 2020, p. 1). As a result, values cannot be ranked ahead of time, nor is there a formula that can simply prescribe the right thing to do. That does not mean, however, that the choices we make are arbitrary. After all, we make these kinds of choices constantly in our everyday lives, and even if there is not one unitary reason for judging one option as superior to another, that does not mean our selection is irrational. One perspective, and the one advanced here, is that rational practical choice requires police to develop a keen sense of what Aristotle calls "perception" or a "sort of complex responsiveness to the salient features" of a concrete situation (Nussbaum 1992, p. 55). Martha Nussbaum provides a close interpretation of this Aristotelian conception of practical rationality that can provide a useful application to frontline police decision-making.

The relevance of making particular judgments in relation to a specific context reminds us how science and policy, while important, provide incomplete guides to the choices we must make. Science might help us understand the best means to a given end, but it cannot tell us which ends matter most. Similarly, policy can provide useful guidance, or an approximate rule of thumb, but general guidelines cannot capture all the particulars of a specific situation relevant to ethical decision-making. In the words of Nussbaum (1992, p. 69):

> The subtleties of a complex ethical situation must be seized in a confrontation with the situation itself, by a faculty that is suited to address it as a complex whole. Prior general formulations lack both the concreteness and the flexibility that is required. They do not contain the particularizing details of the matter at hand, with which decision must grapple; and they are not responsive to what is there, as good decision must be.

Rules can also only capture situations that have been seen before, and thus they cannot encompass all the relevant situational factors that arise in the future. In this sense, Nussbaum argues, decision-makers must be prepared to recognize nonrepeatable or unique features as morally relevant and as "prior to general guidelines" (Nussbaum 1992, p. 90). Obviously, this all requires considerable ethical flexibility, and Aristotle illustrated this flexibility by contrasting it with a person who makes decisions by holding firm to a general rule or law for each situation. Such a person was "Like an architect who tries to use a straight ruler on the intricate curves of a fluted column. No real architect does this. Instead following the lead of the builders of Lesbos he will measure with a flexible strip of metal, the Lesbian rule, that bends to the shape of the stone and is not fixed" (Nussbaum 1992, p. 70).

By identifying several salient values in the neighbor dispute and helping establish that "each is intrinsically valuable, speaking as it were in its own unique voice," a craft model reminds police officers that good judgment requires flexibility, improvisation, and an understanding and consideration of the distinctiveness of each standard (Crowder 2020, p. 1). Understanding that economy, fairness, safety, and so on make unique contributions to the richness of a situation and are not simply interchangeable is important to becoming a reflective and sophisticated decision-maker. Automatically prioritizing safety or efficiency over other salient values is overly reductive. Such a knee-jerk response represents a failure to truly appreciate the "special contribution" of the separateness and distinctiveness of other values and their contribution to the "richness and fullness" of good decision-making, including police work (Nussbaum 1992, p. 60). Doing otherwise can be characterized as evasiveness and fails to recognize that value heterogeneity is an essential component of rational deliberation.

For Aristotle developing the kind of practical wisdom necessary for making good ethical choices relied in large part on experience. The implication is that by confronting a wide range of situations over time, police officers have the opportunity to increase their powers of perception for recognizing the salient characteristics of an encounter and its actors that should be incorporated into their deliberations. Perspicacity is also informed by a decision-maker's capacity to recognize the relevance of a variety of emotions in a particular context. Thus, it is not merely an intellectual endeavor; good judgement is guided by a combination of both the intellect and the emotions:

> Perception *is* a complex response of the entire personality, an appropriate acknowledgment of the features of the situation on which action is based, a *recognition* of the particular. As such, it has in itself non-intellectual components. To have correct perception of the death of a loved one is not simply to take note of this fact with intellect of judgment. If someone noted the fact but was devoid of passional response, we would be inclined to say that he did not really *se, take in, recognize*, what had happened; that he did not acknowledge the situation for what it was. (Nussbaum 1986, p. 309, emphasis in original)

Indeed, Lawrence Sherman (2003), an advocate for more science in policing, has also argued for a more emotionally intelligent form of criminal justice, one that does not just fixate on the rationality of offenders and criminal justice officials.

Finally, Nussbaum suggests that the kind of resourcefulness and responsiveness essential to making discerning moral choices could be illustrated by reading novels. She uses an example from Henry James's *The Golden Bowl*, because it captured "the commitment of Aristotelian practical wisdom to rich descriptions of qualitative heterogeneity, to context-sensitive perceiving, and to emotional and imaginative activity" (Nussbaum 1992, p. 85). Reflecting thoughtfully on specific police–civilian encounters could serve a similar function. To be clear, the argument here is that there is no formal decision-making framework that can account for the "rich contextuality of good choice" (Nussbaum 1992, p. 88), nor did Aristotle provide a straightforward process for how this could be accomplished:

> The perceiving agent can be counted on to investigate and scrutinize the nature of each item and each situation, to respond to what is there before her with full sensitivity and imaginative vigor, not to fall short of what is there to be seen and felt because of evasiveness, scientific abstractness, or a love of simplification. The Aristotelian agent is a person whom we could trust to describe a complex situation with full concreteness of detail and emotional shading, missing nothing of practical relevance. (Nussbaum 1992, p. 84)

Because of its tendency toward abstraction, it helps to illustrate some of the key features of the Aristotelian concept of perception and practical reason in the case of our neighbor dispute.

At the outset, it is striking how the officers in the clip seem to want to resolve the problem as quickly as possible, by suggesting that both parties talk to the building manager, or go to a magistrate to get a summons. They appear to make up their minds about what to do almost immediately, eager to simplify the situation at hand and to avoid the heterogeneity of values it presents. Compared to their rather singular focus on economy (proposing a solution, so they can then quickly leave), they pay less attention to the other salient values of the kind identified by the standards. Aristotle would argue that acting justly requires proper consideration of the intrinsic importance of, say, fairness or problem identification, in all their richness and complexity. From this perspective, focusing on just one value is irrational, and failing to deliberate on others that are relevant is also irrational.

Nor do the officers demonstrate the kind of in-depth perception rooted in a deep appreciation for the nonrepeatable elements of this particular situation. It matters to deciding well that it is these two apartments, in this specific building, on this one night, with these two particular neighbors. These features are morally relevant, but the officers' actions suggest they are defaulting to their usual customary habit of offering brief advice. The complainant says the neighbors "weren't talking for a year," but the officers do not inquire why. She also mentions that the situation is upsetting, and that she has only just come back from the hospital because of a heart condition. Neither officer expresses care or concern about this revelation, or even interest in how these two events might be connected; they simply instruct the complainant to keep her door closed while they approach the second neighbor. In fact, the officers exhibit little empathy during the entire encounter for either neighbor, nor do they try to account for the feelings of hurt and frustration that characterize both neighbors' responses, despite the salience of people's emotions to the process of practical wisdom.

Relationships can be deeply historical, multifaceted, complex, and meaning-laden, and in this dispute, the specific nature of the association between the two neighbors may well have an important bearing on why the second neighbor was so angry and took the door slamming so personally. Rather than moving deftly between any guidance department policy and training may have provided and the relevant features of this particular dispute, the officers appear comfortable following an approach that studiously denies what makes this particular situation and its participants distinct. In some sense they fail to recognize what Aristotle would consider an essential element of ethical decision-making: the recognition of our humanity. From an ethical point of view, it matters that the second neighbor remains steadfast in her belief that she has been wronged by the door slamming. Perhaps she has tried many times to resolve this situation and failed. Seizing upon such specific insights and exploring how they might matter would likely cause the officers to engage in the kind of improvisation and creativity that distinguish the ethical decision-maker.

This application of Aristotle's approach is far from exhaustive, but our purpose is to reveal the priority of specific situational details to ethical deliberation and practical rationality. If this analysis seems peculiar or jarring in a monograph on policing, it is worth reflecting on why this is the case. As Nussbaum similarly observes about applying examples from literature to philosophy, perhaps it is because we desire straightforward guidance on how to make good decisions in these kinds of situations, without a fuller understanding of the considerable complexity they hold. But there is no general formula for this process and "no safe guarantee at all," as good ethical decision-making requires the "moral effort of straining to see correctly and to come up with the appropriate picture or description" (Nussbaum 1992, pp. 88, 97). For some this is likely to be disappointing and frustrating, but for Aristotle choosing well was about perception and flexibility in addressing a situation as a complex whole. Ethics could never have the "precision of science" and to rely on some kind of decision-making rule or formal theory to make things less demanding on the decision-maker and those judging their choices was a sign of "immaturity and weakness" (Nussbaum 1992, pp. 71, 74). But that did not mean that any decisions were ad hoc. The lessons from lived experience coupled with training and guidance from ethical principles, and a mindful capacity to adapt laws and policies to situational exigencies, help guide a deliberative process for improving ethical and wise judgment, even if there is no single indisputable answer to what decision is best. What is clear is that if we desire police officers capable of practical wisdom, Aristotle provides a perspective whose relationship to science and bureaucracy and other models for governing discretion merits our attention.

We are unsure to what extent the model we describe here is currently being used by police agencies in the United States. We suspect that certain features of police administration and operations, such as BWC policies and reviews of use-of-force incidents, include some learning opportunities for reflection and improvement (see, for example, Thacher 2020). At the same time, we doubt there are examples of all facets of this model operating as part of a comprehensive, inclusive, and sustained approach to guiding patrol officer decision-making.

When it comes to coaching, experiential learning, reflection, and making value judgments, policing would appear to be lagging behind other fields, such as medicine, teaching, and even corrections. For example, the current dominant approach to working with probationers requires officers to use a variety of professional skills that can only be developed via experiential learning and continuous coaching (Toronjo 2019, 2020). Research suggests coaching probation officers is a promising practice, which can help improve both officer practice and probationer outcomes (Bonta and Andrews 2016). These coaching models in probation take inspiration from reflective practice models used in other "helping professions" such as nursing, social work, and teaching, and aim to train frontline supervisors as coaches.

The question naturally arises, how might police agencies begin to incorporate the craft learning model into police training and practice? Space constraints prevent us from providing detailed implementation guidelines, but the following factors are likely to be important to its successful adoption. First, because of its focus on street-level policing, the continuous participation and feedback of lower-ranking officers at all stages of the planning and implementation process is crucial. As others have argued, involving organizational members at all levels "helps reduce barriers to change by creating psychological ownership, promoting the dissemination of critical information, and encouraging employee feedback for fine-tuning the change during implementation" (Fernandez and Rainey 2006, p. 170). To help convince officers of craft's utility, leadership must engage directly in a meaningful dialogue that helps take account of officers' existing knowledge and beliefs. This process might also contribute to the credibility and legitimacy of researchers facilitating implementation. By collaborating actively with patrol officers as equals rather than simply imposing change upon them, it is more likely that researchers' viewpoints will be taken seriously. Persuasion involves far more than just presenting a clear and logical argument for a desired change (Van de Ven and Schomaker 2002, p. 90). This dialogue would also be an opportunity for departments to learn how to adapt the learning model to its unique local context by taking into account the department's specific organizational history and its relationship to its own community (Thacher 2020).

In addition to building internal support, departments would benefit from the support of local government politicians, such as mayors and city managers, and key external stakeholders, who might also advocate for additional resources for overtime or training. Regarding the latter, the National Institute of Justice could consider funding demonstration projects that might encourage some police departments to pilot the craft learning model on a small scale within their agencies to see if it is a viable option, particularly in relation to other department subsystems (e.g., existing supervisory practices) before a larger rollout. Research suggests that funding can be an important factor for innovation adoption (Katz, Maguire, and Roncek 2002). Finally, these demonstration projects could be subjected to a rigorous evaluation of their processes and effects.

5 Conclusion

At the heart of this Element lies one question: How do we best prepare patrol officers to make good choices in situations that are ambiguous and complex? After all, we ask this same question about other similarly positioned professionals: How do we best prepare surgeons or social workers, who must consider many situational details when deciding what to do in a particular case, and who must navigate the knotty problem of conflicting values? Certainly, scientific knowledge and medical guidelines can offer useful guidance, but we doubt that the recipients of these services would be fully satisfied, if these were the only means of ensuring good performance. If we were in the position of a patient, or a client, relying on the judiciousness of the professional whose services we sought, we would likely also wish for a practitioner with the kind of knowledge and skills that can only be gained by grappling with a wide range of difficult cases and a rigorous process of practical reflection. We argue that this knowledge is fundamentally important to making good choices, but in policing it is currently undervalued and underexplored.

To be clear, we are not advocating that craft replace other forms of governing discretion, but that reformers and scholars make better use of craft's potential for guiding police policy and practice. One way, and the approach we describe here, is to try and identify standards for different types of prototypical police–civilian encounters. These could provide a framework for directing attention to some of the most relevant situational factors for deciding what to do while also taking into account the realities of actual police work. These can then provide a basis for deeper inquiry into the practicalities and possibilities of various alternatives and their ethical implications. By requiring that officers confront the reasons for their choices directly it can also help strengthen accountability in an area that remains relatively untouched, even with the diffusion of BWCs.

Of the systems for regulating or governing discretion, craft has probably received the least attention from today's reformers. We articulate the strengths and weaknesses of each of these systems to suggest that the greatest benefits to police discretion would seem to accrue from incorporating some combination of all five for the mutual aim and commitment to improving street-level perform-ance. An overreliance on only some of these systems means that valuable opportunities for advancing meaningful reform remain underdeveloped. For example, an overreliance on laws and rules can result in formulaic or narrow-minded judgments, and a commitment to craft while being overly dismissive of science can result in adopting practices that do not work as intended. The community as a source of guidance and insight can also be too easily ignored in favor of control systems that rest within the direct control of the police organization. What is worth seeking is a blend of these systems that would allow for the strengths of each to compensate for the weaknesses of others.

Centuries ago, Aristotle proposed that all virtues were a mean between two vices: one of deficiency and one of excess. Thus, courage in the face of danger was moderation between the moral deficiency of cowardice and the moral excess of hubris. Similarly, channeling discretion to maximize police perform-ance without inviting undue risk, stifling creativity, or encouraging bad judg-ment requires careful attention to craft's capacity to improve perception and discernment as well as to the guidance offered by law, bureaucracy, science, and the concerns of the community. For those particularly concerned about the danger of softening the "coercive potential" of administrative rules in order to deter bad police work, the actual need for coercion could be reduced by the adoption of a craft learning model because of the involvement of patrol officers and the community in a shared moral commitment to better policing (Mastrofski and Greene 1993, p. 89).

The vision we present here represents a bold endeavor, but the current crisis in policing may be an opportunity for new and creative responses to police reform. According to a 2022 Gallup Poll of US adults, 50 percent of respondents reported that "major changes are needed to make policing better" compared to 11 percent who said no changes were necessary. To paraphrase Carl Klockars (1985, p. 119), if we really value police professionalism, how might we then trust the police and teach them to use their powers wisely in the same way that we must trust and teach similar professionals in whom we have no choice but to entrust equally formidable powers? Our hope is that what we suggest here will stimulate other advocates of police reform to address this question, perhaps even testing and refining the model we propose here for making decision-making more reflective, transparent, and principled.

References

Abner, G., & Rush, S. (2022). Assessing the correlates of CALEA accreditation: A state-of-the-art review. *Policing: An International Journal*, *45*(5), 776–793. https://doi.org/10.1108/pijpsm-02-2022-0032.

Alpert, G., & Rojek, J. (2011). *Frontline police officer assessments of risks and decision-making during encounters with offenders*. Briefing paper: ARC Center of Excellence in Policing and Security.

Angell, J. E. (1971). Toward an alternative to the police classic organizational arrangements: A democratic model. *Criminology*, *9*(2–3), 185–206. https://doi.org/10.1111/j.1745-9125.1971.tb00766.x.

Baldwin, J. (1966, July 11). A report from occupied territory. *The Nation*. https://www.thenation.com/article/culture/report-occupied-territory/

Barbee, A. P., Christensen, D., Antle, B., Wandersman, A., & Cahn, K. (2011). Successful adoption and implementation of a comprehensive casework practice model in a public child welfare agency: Application of the Getting to Outcomes (GTO) model. *Children and Youth Services Review*, *33*(5), 622–633. https://doi.org/10.1016/j.childyouth.2010.11.008.

Bass, B. M., & Avolio, B. J. (1994). *Improving Organizational Effectiveness through Transformational Leadership*. Thousand Oaks: Sage.

Bayley, D. H. (1986). The tactical choices of police patrol officers. *Journal of Criminal Justice*, *14*(4), 329–348.

Bayley, D. H. (1994). *Police for the Future*. Oxford: Oxford University Press.

Bayley, D. H. (2008). Police reform: Who done it? *Policing and Society*, *18*(1), 7–17. https://doi.org/10.1080/10439460701718518.

Bayley, D. H. (2016). The complexities of 21st century policing. *Policing*, *10*(3), 163–170. https://doi.org/10.1093/police/paw019.

Bayley, D. H., & Bittner, E. (1984). Learning the skills of policing. *Law and Contemporary Problems*, *47*(4), 35–59. https://doi.org/10.2307/1191686.

Bayley, D. H., & Garofalo J. (1989). The management of violence by police patrol officers. *Criminology* *27*(1), 1–26.

Berrey, E., Hoffman, S. G., & Nielsen, L. B. (2012). Situated justice: A contextual analysis of fairness and inequality in employment discrimination litigation. *Law & Society Review*, *46*(1), 1–36. https://doi.org/10.1111/j.1540-5893.2012.00471.x.

Bittner, E. (1967). The police on skid-row: A study of peace-keeping. *American Sociological Review*, *32*(5), 699–715.

Bittner, E. (1967a). Police discretion in emergency apprehension of mentally ill persons. *Social Problems, 14*(3), 278–292. https://doi.org/10.1525/sp.1967.14.3 .03a00040.

Bittner, E. (1970). *The Functions of the Police in Modern Society.* National Institute of Mental Health.

Bittner, E. (1983). Legality and workmanship: Introduction to control in the police organization. In M. Punch (Ed.), *Control in the Police Organization* (pp. 1–11). MIT Press.

Bittner, E. (1990). *Aspects of Police Work.* Northeastern University Press.

Blumberg, D. M., Schlosser, M. D., Papazoglou, K., Creighton, S., & Kaye, C. C. (2019). New directions in police academy training: A call to action. *International Journal of Environmental Research and Public Health, 16*(24), 4941. https://doi.org/10.3390/ijerph16244941.

Bonta, J., & Andrews, D. A. (2016). *The Psychology of Criminal Conduct* (6th ed.). Routledge, Taylor & Francis Group.

Braga, A. A., & Weisburd, D. L. (2020). Does hot spots policing have meaningful impacts on crime? Findings from an alternative approach to estimating effect sizes from place-based program evaluations. *Journal of Quantitative Criminology,* 1–22. https://doi.org/10.1007/s10940-020-09481-7.

Brown, M. K. (1981). *Working the Street.* Russell Sage Foundation.

Charles, M. T. (2000). *Police Training–Breaking All the Rules: Implementing the Adult Education Model into Police Training.* Charles C. Thomas Publication.

Cheng, T. (2022). The cumulative discretion of police over community complaints. *American Journal of Sociology, 127*(6), 1782–1817. https://doi .org/10.1086/719682.

Christopher, S. (2015). The police service can be a critical reflective practice . . . If it wants. *Policing, 9*(4), 326–339. https://doi.org/10.1093/police/pav007.

Cobb, J. (2021, August 19). A Warning Ignored. *The New York Review of Books.* www.nybooks.com/articles/2021/08/19/kerner-commission-warning-ignored/.

Cohen, H. S., & Feldberg, M. (1991). *Power and Restraint: The Moral Dimension of Police Work.* Praeger.

Cordner, G. (2017). Police culture: Individual and organizational differences in police officer perspectives. *Policing: An International Journal of Police Strategies & Management, 40*(1), 11–25. https://doi.org/10.1108/pijpsm-07-2016-0116.

Couper, D. C., & Lobitz, S. H. (1991). *Quality Policing: The Madison Experience.* Police Executive Research Forum.

Crowder, G. (2020). *The Problem of Value Pluralism: Isaiah Berlin and beyond.* Routledge.

Dagan, D. (2017. November 25). The Baltimore Cops studying Plato and James Baldwin. *The Atlantic.* www.theatlantic.com/politics/archive/2017/11/the-baltimore-cops-studying-plato-and-james-baldwin/546485/.

Davis, K. C. (1969). *Discretionary Justice.* Louisiana State University Press.

Davis, K. C. (1975). *Police Discretion.* West.

Dewey, J. (1933). *How We Think: A Restatement of the Relation of Reflective Thinking to the Educative Process.* D.C. Heath and Co. Publishers.

Ellinger, A. D., & Bostrom, R. P. (1999). Managerial coaching behaviors in learning organizations. *Journal of Management Development, 18*(9), 752–771. https://doi.org/10.1108/02621719910300810.

Engel, R. S. (2002). Patrol officer supervision in the community policing era. *Journal of Criminal Justice, 30*(1), 51–64. https://doi.org/10.1016/s0047-2352(01)00122-2.

Engel, R. S., & Worden, R. E. (2003). Police officers' attitudes, behavior, and supervisory influences: An analysis of problem solving. *Criminology, 41*(1), 131–166.

Ervin, N. E. (2005). Clinical coaching: A strategy for enhancing evidence-based nursing practice. *Clinical Nurse Specialist CNS, 19*(6), 296–301. https://doi.org/10.4161/cc.4.12.2282.

Etizoni, A. (1975). *A Comparative Analysis of Complex Organizations.* Free Press.

Feldman, D. C., & Lankau, M. J. (2005). Executive coaching: A review and agenda for future research. *Journal of Management, 31*(6), 829–848. https://doi.org/10.1177/0149206305279599.

Fernandez, S., & Rainey, H. G. (2006). Managing successful organizational change in the public sector. *Public Administration Review, 66*(2), 168–176.

Fielding, N. (1984). Police socialization and police competence. *The British Journal of Sociology, 35*(4), 568. https://doi.org/10.2307/590435.

Flyvbjerg, B. (2012). Making social science matter. In G. Papanagnou (Ed.), *Social Science and Policy Challenges: Democracy, Values, and Capacities* (pp. 25–56). Unesco.

Flyvbjerg, B., & Sampson, S. (2001). *Making Social Science Matter Why Social Inquiry Fails and How It Can Succeed Again.* Cambridge University Press.

Folger, R., & Cropanzano, R. (2001). Fairness theory: Justice as accountability. In J. Greenberg & R. Cropanzano (Eds.), *Advances in Organization Justice* (pp. 1–55). Stanford University Press.

Force, P. A. T. (2016). *Recommendations for Reform: Restoring Trust between the Chicago Police and the Communities They Serve*. Chicago Police Accountability Task Force.

Friedman, B. (2017). *Unwarranted: Policing without Permission*. Farrar, Straus & Giroux.

Gau, J. M., & Brunson, R. K. (2010). Procedural justice and order maintenance policing: A study of inner-city young men's perceptions of police legitimacy. *Justice Quarterly, 27*(2), 255–279. https://doi.org/10.1080/0741882090 2763889.

Gawande, A. (2011, September 26). Personal Best. *The New Yorker*. www .newyorker.com/magazine/2011/10/03/personal-best.

Gawande, A. (2016, June 10). The Mistrust of Science. *The New Yorker*. www .newyorker.com/news/news-desk/the-mistrust-of-science.

Goldstein, H. (1963). Police discretion: The ideal versus the real. *Public Administration Review, 23*(3), 140. https://doi.org/10.2307/973838.

Goldstein, H. (1967). Police policy formulation: A proposal for improving police performance. *Michigan Law Review, 65*(6), 1123. https://doi.org/ 10.2307/1287280.

Goldstein, H. (1977). *Policing a Free Society*. Ballinger.

Goldstein, H. (1979). Improving policing: A problem-oriented approach. *Crime & Delinquency, 25*(2), 236–258.

Goldstein, H. (1990). *Problem-Oriented Policing*. McGraw-Hill.

Gould, J. B., & Mastrofski, S. D. (2004). Suspect searches: Assessing police behavior under the U.S. Constitution. *Criminology and Public Policy, 3*(3), 315–362. https://doi.org/10.1111/j.1745-9133.2004.tb00046.x.

Gouldner, A. (1954). *Patterns of Industrial Bureaucracy*. The Free Press.

Greene, J. R. (2014). New directions in policing: Balancing prediction and meaning in police research. *Justice Quarterly, 31*(2), 193–228. https://doi .org/10.1080/07418825.2013.840389.

Haidt, J. (2001). The emotional dog and its rational tail: A social intuitionist approach to moral judgment. *Psychological Review, 108*(4), 814–834. https:// doi.org/10.1037//0033-295x.108.4.814.

Harmon, R. A. (2016). Why arrest? *Michigan Law Review, 115*(3), 307–364.

Harmon, R. A. (2021). *The Law of Police*. Wolters Kluwer.

Hart, H. M. (1958). The aims of the criminal law. *Law and Contemporary Problems, 23*(3), 401–441. https://doi.org/10.2307/1190221.

Heffernan, W. C., & Lovely, R. W. (1991). Evaluating the fourth amendment exclusionary rule: The problem of police compliance with the law. *University of Michigan Journal of Law Reform, 24*, 311–369.

Herbert, S. (1998). Police subculture reconsidered. *Criminology, 36*(2), 343–370. https://doi.org/10.1111/j.1745-9125.1998.tb01251.x.

Ibrahim, A. M., Varban, O. A., & Dimick, J. B. (2016). Novel uses of video to accelerate the surgical learning curve. *Journal of Laparoendoscopic & Advanced Surgical Techniques, 26*(4), 240–242. https://doi.org/10.1089/lap.2016.0100.

Jonathan-Zamir, T., Weisburd, D., Dayan, M., & Zisso, M. (2019). The proclivity to rely on professional experience and evidence-based policing: Findings from a survey of high-ranking officers in the Israel police. *Criminal Justice and Behavior, 46*(10), 1456–1474. https://doi.org/10.1177/0093854819842903.

Joyce, B. R., & Showers, B. (2002). *Student Achievement Through Staff Development* (Vol. 3). Association for Supervision and Curriculum Development.

Kahneman, D., & Klein, G. (2009). Conditions for intuitive expertise: A failure to disagree. *American Psychologist, 64*(6), 515–526. https://doi.org/10.1037/a0016755.

Katz, C. M., Maguire, E. R., & Roncek, D. W. (2002). The creation of specialized police gang units: A macro-level analysis of contingency, social threat, and resource dependency explanations. *Policing: An International Journal of Police Strategies and Management, 25*(3), 472–506.

Kelling, G. L. (1999). *Broken Windows and Police Discretion*. U.S. Department of Justice. www.ojp.gov/pdffiles1/nij/178259.pdf.

Kelling, G. L., & Moore, M. H. (1988). *The Evolving Strategy of Policing* (No. 4). U.S. Department of Justice, Office of Justice Programs, National Institute of Justice.

Klein, G. (2015). A naturalistic decision-making perspective on studying intuitive decision-making. *Journal of Applied Research in Memory and Cognition, 4*(3), 164–168. https://doi.org/10.1016/j.jarmac.2015.07.001.

Klein, G. A. (2011). *Streetlights and Shadows: Searching for the Keys to Adaptive Decision-making*. MIT Press.

Klein, G., Calderwood, R., & Clinton-Cirocco, A. (2010). Rapid decision-making on the fire ground: The original study plus a postscript. *Journal of Cognitive Engineering and Decision-making, 4*(3), 186–209. https://doi.org/10.1518/155534310x12844000801203.

Kleinig, J. (2005). *The Ethics of Policing*. Cambridge University Press.

Klockars, C. B. (1985). *Idea of Police*. Sage.

Klockars, C. B., Ivković, S. K., & Haberfeld, M. R. (2005). Enhancing police integrity. U.S. Department of Justice: Office of Justice Programs.

Koen, M., & Mathna, B. (2019). Body-worn cameras and internal accountability at a police agency. *American Journal of Qualitative Research, 3*(2), 1–22. https://doi.org/10.29333/ajqr/6363.

Koen, M. C., Newell, B. C., & Roberts, M. R. (2021). Body-worn cameras: Technological frames and project abandonment. *Journal of Criminal Justice, 72*, 101773. https://doi.org/10.1016/j.jcrimjus.2020.101773.

Kolb, D. A. (2014). *Experiential Learning: Experience as the Source of Learning and Development*. FT Press.

Krantz, S. (1979). *Police Policymaking: The Boston Experience*. Lexington Books.

Laub, J. H. (2004). The life course of criminology in the United States: The American society of criminology 2003 Presidential Address. *Criminology, 42*(1), 1–26. https://doi.org/10.1111/j.1745-9125.2004.tb00511.x.

Loftus, B. (2010). Police occupational culture: Classic themes, altered times. *Policing and Society, 20*(1), 1–20. https://doi.org/10.1080/10439460903281547.

Loftus, B. (2022). *Police Culture: Origins, Features, and Reform*. Mass Casualty Commission. https://masscasualtycommission.ca/files/commissioned-reports/COMM0053825.pdf?t=1652281766.

Lum, C. (2009). *Translating Police Research into Practice: Ideas in American Policing*. The Police Foundation.

Lum, C. M., & Koper, C. S. (2017). *Evidence-Based Policing: Translating Research into Practice*. Oxford University Press.

Lum, C., Koper, C. S., Wilson, D. B., et al. (2020). Body-worn cameras' effects on police officers and citizen behavior: A systematic review. *Campbell Systematic Reviews, 16*(3), 1–40. https://doi.org/10.1002/cl2.1112.

Lum, C., Koper, C. S., & Wu, X. (2021). Can we really defund the police? A nine-agency study of police response to calls for service. *Police Quarterly, 25*(3), 1–26. https://doi.org/10.1177/10986111211035002.

Lvovsky, A. (2021). Rethinking police expertise. *Yale Law Journal, 131*(2), 475–572.

Manning, P. K. (1997). *Police Work: The Social Organization of Policing*. Waveland Press.

Mastrofski, S. D. (1988). Community policing as reform: A cautionary tale. In J. R. Greene & S. D. Mastrofski (Eds.), *Community Policing: Rhetoric or Reality* (pp. 47–67). Praeger.

Mastrofski, S. D. (1996). Measuring police performance in public encounters. In L. T. Hoover (Ed.), *Quantifying Quality in Policing* (pp. 207–241). Police Executive Research Forum.

Mastrofski, S. D. (1999). *Policing for People: Ideas in American Policing*. Police Foundation.

Mastrofski, S. D. (2000). The police in America. In J. F. Sheley (Ed.), *Criminology: A Contemporary Handbook* (pp. 405–443). Wadsworth/Thomson Learning.

Mastrofski, S. D. (2004). Controlling street-level police discretion. *The ANNALS of the American Academy of Political and Social Science, 593*(1), 100–118. https://doi.org/10.1177/0002716203262584.

Mastrofski, S. D. (2018). *Do the Right Thing: Evaluating Police Performance at the Street Level.* Inaugural Stephen D. Mastrofski Lecture.

Mastrofski, S. D. (2019). Community policing: A skeptical view. In D. Weisburd & A. A. Braga (Eds.), *Police Innovation: Contrasting Perspectives* (pp. 44–73). Cambridge University Press.

Mastrofski, S. D., & Greene, J. R. (1993). Community policing and the rule of law. In D. Weisburd & C. Uchida (Eds.), *Police Innovation and Control of the Police* (pp. 80–102). Springer-Verlag.

Mastrofski, S. D., & Ritti, R. R. (2000). Making sense of community policing: A theory-based analysis. *Police Practice and Research, 1*(2), 183–210.

Mastrofski, S. D., Snipes, J. B., Parks, R. B., & Maxwell, C. D. (2000). The helping hand of the law: Police control of citizens on request. *Criminology, 38*(2), 307–342. https://doi.org/10.1111/j.1745-9125.2000.tb00892.x.

Mastrofski, S. D., Snipes, J. B., & Supina, A. E. (1996). Compliance on demand: The public's response to specific police requests. *Journal of Research in Crime and Delinquency, 33*(3), 269–305. https://doi.org/10.1177/0022427896033003001.

Mastrofski, S. D., & Uchida, C. D. (1993). Transforming the police. *Journal of Research in Crime and Delinquency, 30*(3), 330–358. https://doi.org/10.1177/0022427893030003005.

Mastrofski, S. D., & Willis, J. J. (2010). Police organization continuity and change: Into the twenty-first century. *Crime and Justice, 39*(1), 55–144. https://doi.org/10.1086/653046.

Meares, T., Tyler, T., & Gardener, J. (2015). Lawful or fair? How cops and laypeople perceive good policing. *Journal of Criminal Law and Criminology, 105*(2), 297–344. https://scholarlycommons.law.northwestern.edu/jclc/vol105/iss2/1.

Miller, W. R., & Rollnick, S. (2012). *Motivational Interviewing* (3rd ed.). Guilford Press.

Milne, D. (2009). *Evidence-Based Clinical Supervision Principles and Practice.* BPS Blackwell.

Moore, M. H. (1995). Learning while doing: Linking knowledge to policy in the development of community policing and violence prevention in the United States. In P. O. Wilkstrom, R. V. Clarke & J. McCord (Eds.), *Integrating*

Crime Prevention Strategies: Propensity and Opportunity (pp. 301–333). The National Council for Crime Prevention.

Muir, W. K. Jr. (1977). *Police: Streetcorner Politicians*. University of Chicago Press.

Neyroud, P., & Weisburd, D. (2023). Re-inventing policing: Using science to transform policing. In D. L. Weisburd, T. Jonathan-Zamir, G. Perry & B. Hasisi. *The Future of Evidence-Based Policing* (pp. 44–63). Cambridge University Press.

Nix, J., Todak, N., & Tregle, B. (2020). Understanding body-worn camera diffusion in U.S. policing. *Police Quarterly, 23*(3), 396–422. https://doi .org/10.21428/cb6ab371.ffc93ca8.

Nussbaum, M. (1986). *The Fragility of Goodness: Luck and Ethics in Greek Tragedy and Philosophy*. Cambridge University Press.

Nussbaum, M. C. (1992). *Love's Knowledge: Essays on Philosophy and Literature*. Oxford University Press.

Ohlin, L. E. (1993). Surveying discretion by criminal justice decision makers. In L. E. Ohlin & F. J. Remington (Eds.), *Discretion in Criminal Justice: The Tension Between Individualization and Uniformity* (pp. 1–22). State University of New York Press.

Owens, E., Weisburd, D., Amendola, K. L., & Alpert, G. P. (2018). Can you build a better cop? *Criminology & Public Policy, 17*(1), 41–87. https://doi.org/ 10.1111/1745-9133.12337.

Paoline, E. A. (2003). Taking stock: Toward a richer understanding of police culture. *Journal of Criminal Justice, 31*(3), 199–214. https://doi.org/10.1016/ s0047-2352(03)00002-3.

Parks, R. B., Mastrofski, S. D., DeJong, C., & Gray, M. K. (1999). How officers spend their time with the community. *Justice Quarterly, 16*(3), 483–518. https://doi.org/10.1080/07418829900094241.

Pennington, L., & Farrell, A. (2019). Role of voice in the legal process*. *Criminology, 57*(2), 343–368. https://doi.org/10.1111/1745-9125.12205.

Perry, S., Hasisi, B., & Weisburd, D. (2023). "The contribution of the 'super evidence cop:' Key role of police leaders in advancing evidence-based policing". In A. Verma & D. K Das (Eds.), *Police Leaders as Thinkers* (pp. 105–117). Springer. https://doi.org/10.1007/978-3-031-19700-0.

Phelps, J. M., Strype, J., Le Bellu, S., Lahlou, S., & Aandal, J. (2016). Experiential learning and simulation-based training in Norwegian police education: Examining body-worn video as a tool to encourage reflection. *Policing*, 1–16. https://doi.org/10.1093/police/paw014.

Ponomarenko, M. (2019). Rethinking police rulemaking. *Northwestern University Law Review, 144*(1), 1–64. https://doi.org/10.2139/ssrn.3333804.

President's Commission on Law Enforcement and Administration of Justice. (1967). *The Challenge of Crime in a Free Society*. United States Government Printing Office.

President's Taskforce on 21st Century Policing: Final Report. (2015). Office of Community-Oriented Policing Services. https://cops.usdoj.gov/pdf/task force/taskforce_finalreport.pdf

Rahr, S., & Rice, S. K. (2015). *From Warriors to Guardians*. U.S. Department of Justice, Office of Justice Programs, National Institute of Justice.

Ramsey, C. H. (2014). *The Challenge of Policing in a Democratic Society: A Personal Journey Toward Understanding*. Harvard Kennedy School Program in Criminal Justice Policy and Management.

Sabel, C. F., & Simon W. H. (2016). The duty of responsible administration and the problem of police accountability. *Yale Journal on Regulation, 33*(1), 165–214.

Salas, E., Rosen, M. A., & DiazGranados, D. (2010). Expertise-based intuition and decision-making in organizations. *Journal of Management, 36*(4), 941–973. https://doi.org/10.1177/0149206309350084

Schön, D. A. (1983). *The Reflective Practitioner: How Professionals Think in Action*. Basic Books.

Schön, D. A. (1987). *Educating the Reflective Practitioner: Toward a New Design for Teaching and Learning*. Josey-Bass.

Searcey, D. (2020). What would efforts to defund or disband police departments really mean? *The New York Times*. www.nytimes.com/2020/06/08/us/what-does-defund-police-mean.html.

Sennett, R. (2008). *The Craftsman*. Yale University Press.

Sherman, L. W. (1984). Experiments in police discretion: Scientific boon or dangerous knowledge? *Law and Contemporary Problems, 47*(4), 61. https://doi.org/10.2307/1191687.

Sherman, L. W. (1998). *Evidence-Based Policing: Ideas in American Policing*. Police Foundation.

Sherman, L. W. (2003). Reason for emotion: Reinventing justice with theories, innovation, and research. *Criminology, 41*(1), 1–38. https://doi.org/10.1111/j.1745-9125.2003.tb00980.x.

Simmel, G. (1908/1950). The stranger. In K. H. Wolff (Ed.), *The Sociology of Georg Simmel* (pp. 402–408). The Free Press.

Sklansky, D. A. (2008). *Democracy and the Police*. Stanford University Press.

Sklansky, D. A., & Marks, M. (2008). The role of the rank and file in police reform. *Policing and Society, 18*(1), 1–6. https://doi.org/10.1080/10439460 701718484.

Skogan, W. G. (2006). *Police and Community in Chicago: A Tale of Three Cities*. Oxford: Oxford University Press.

Skogan, W. G. (2019). The promise of community policing. In D. Weisburd & A. A. Braga (Eds.), *Police Innovation: Contrasting Perspectives* (pp. 28–43).

Skogan, W. G., & Frydl, K. . (2004). *Fairness and Effectiveness in Policing the Evidence*. National Academies Press.

Skogan, W. G., & Meares, T. L. (2004). Lawful policing. *The ANNALS of the American Academy of Political and Social Science*, *593*(1), 66–83. https://doi.org/10.1177/0002716204263637.

Skogan, W. G., & Roth, J. A. (2004). Introduction. In W. G. Skogan (Ed.), *Community Policing (Can it Work?)* (pp. xvii–xxxiv). Thomson/Wadsworth.

Sloan III, J. J., & Paoline III, E. A. (2021). "They need more training!" A national level analysis of police academy basic training priorities. *Police Quarterly*, *24*(4), 109861112110133. https://doi.org/10.1177/1098611121 1013311.

Snyder, J. A., Crow, M. S., & Smykla, J. O. (2019). Police officer and supervisor perceptions of body-worn cameras pre- and postimplementation: The importance of officer buy-in. *Criminal Justice Review*, *44*(3), 322–338. https://doi .org/10.1177/0734016819846223.

Sparrow, M. K. (2011). *Governing Science*. Harvard Kennedy School Program in Criminal Justice Policy and Management.

Stalans, L. J., & Finn, M. A. (1995). How novice and experienced officers interpret wife assaults: Normative and efficiency frames. *Law & Society Review*, *29*(2), 287. https://doi.org/10.2307/3054013.

Stoughton, S. W., Alpert, G. P., and Noble, J. (2015). Why police need constructive criticism. *The Atlantic*. www.theatlantic.com/politics/archive/2015/ 12/officer-porter-mistrial-police-culture/421656/.

Telep, C. W., & Lum, C. (2014). The receptivity of officers to empirical research and evidence-based policing: An examination of survey data from three agencies. *Police Quarterly*, *17*(4), 359–385. https://doi.org/10.1177/10986111 14548099.

Thacher, D. (2001). Policing is not a treatment: Alternatives to the medical model of police research. *Journal of Research in Crime and Delinquency*, *38*(4), 387–415. https://doi.org/10.1177/0022427801038004003.

Thacher, D. (2004). Order maintenance reconsidered: Moving beyond strong causal reasoning. *The Journal of Criminal Law and Criminology (1973-)*, *94*(2), 381–414. https://doi.org/10.2307/3491374.

Thacher, D. (2006). The normative case study. *American Journal of Sociology*, *111*(6), 1631–1676. https://doi.org/10.1086/499913.

Thacher, D. (2008). Research for the front lines. *Policing and Society, 18*(1), 46–59. https://doi.org/10.1080/10439460701718567.

Thacher, D. (2016). Channeling police discretion: The hidden potential of focused deterrence. *University of Chicago Legal Forum, 13*, 533–577. http://chicagounbound.uchicago.edu/uclf/vol2016/iss1/13.

Thacher, D. (2019). The aspiration of scientific policing. *Law & Social Inquiry, 44*(1), 273–297. https://doi.org/10.1111/lsi.12367.

Thacher, D. (2020). The learning model of use-of-force reviews. *Law & Social Inquiry, 45*(3), 755–786. https://doi.org/10.1017/lsi.2019.80.

Thacher, D. (2022). Shrinking the police footprint. *Criminal Justice Ethics*, 1–24. https://doi.org/10.1080/0731129x.2022.2062546.

Thacher, D., & Rein, M. (2004). Managing value conflict in public policy. *Governance, 17*(4), 457–486. https://doi.org/10.1111/j.0952-1895.2004.00254.x.

Toronjo, H. (2019). Gut check: Turning experience into knowledge. In P. Ugwudike, H. Graham, F. McNeill, P. Raynor, F. S. Taxman, & C. Trotter (Eds.), *The Routledge Companion to Rehabilitative Work in Criminal Justice* (pp. 352–382). Routledge.

Toronjo, H. (2020). *Do you really want to help me? Practitioner perspectives on a new coaching model for probation front-line supervisors*. MA Thesis, Department of Criminology, Law and Society: George Mason University.

Tyler, T. R. (2004). Enhancing police legitimacy. *The ANNALS of the American Academy of Political and Social Science, 593*, 84–99.

Tyler, T. R., Callahan, P. E., & Frost, J. (2007). Armed, and dangerous (?): Motivating rule adherence among agents of social control. *Law & Society Review, 41*(2), 457–492. https://doi.org/10.1111/j.1540-5893.2007.00304.x.

Van de Ven, A. H., & Schomaker, M. S. (2002). Commentary: The rhetoric of evidence-based medicine. *Health Care Management Review, 27*(3), 88–91.

Vanecko, R. (2020). The Chicago Consent Decree and the Fallacy of Police Reform. *Available at SSRN 3724453*.

Van Maanen, J. (1983). The boss: First-line supervision in an American police agency. In M. Punch (Ed.), *Control in the Police Organization* (pp. 275–317). MIT Press.

Waddington, P. A. J., Williams, K., Wright, M., & Newburn, T. (2015). Dissension in public evaluations of the police. *Policing and Society, 25*(2), 212–235.

Walker, S. (1992). Origins of the contemporary criminal justice paradigm: The American bar foundation survey, 1953–1969. *Justice Quarterly, 9*(1), 47–76.

Walker, S. (1993). *Taming the System: The Control of Discretion in Criminal Justice: 1950–1990*. Oxford University Press.

Walker, S. (1993a). Historical roots of the legal control of police behavior. In D. Weisburd & C. Uchida (Eds.), *Police Innovation and Control of the Police* (pp. 32–55). Springer-Verlag.

Walker, S. (2016). Governing the American police: Wrestling with the problems of democracy. *University of Chicago Legal Forum, 15*, 615–660.

Walker, S., & Archbold, C. (2014). *The New World of Police Accountability.* Sage.

Walkers, S., & Katz, C. M. (2005). *The Police in America: An Introduction.* McGraw-Hill.

Wasserman, R., & Moore, M. H. (1988). *Values in Policing* (No. 8). U.S. Department of Justice, Office of Justice Programs, National Institute of Justice.

Weisburd, D. L. (2003). Ethical practice and evaluation of interventions in crime and justice. *Evaluation Review, 27*(3), 336–354. https://doi.org/10.1177/0193 841x03027003007.

Weisburd, D. L. (2015). The law of crime concentration and the criminology of place. *Criminology, 53*(2), 133–157. https://doi.org/10.1111/1745-9125.12070.

Weisburd, D. L., Mastrofski, S. D., McNally, A. M., Greenspan, R., & Willis, J. J. (2003). Reforming to preserve: Compstat and strategic problem solving in American policing. *Criminology Public Policy, 2*(3), 421–456. https://doi .org/10.1111/j.1745-9133.2003.tb00006.x.

Weisburd, D. L., Jonathan-Zamir, T., Perry, G., & Hasisi, B. (2023). The future of evidence-based policing: Introduction. In D. L. Weisburd, T. Jonathan-Zamir, G. Perry, & B. Hasisi. *The Future of Evidence-Based Policing.* Cambridge University Press.

Weisburd, D. L., Telep, C. W., Vovak, H., Zastrow, T., Braga, A. A., & Turchan, B. (2022). Reforming the police through procedural justice training: A multicity randomized trial at crime hot spots. *Proceedings of the National Academy of Sciences, 119*(14), 1–6.

White, M. D., & Malm, A. E. (2020). *Cops, Cameras, and Crisis: The Potential and the Perils of Police Body-Worn Cameras.* New York University Press.

White, M., Fradella, H., & Flippin, M. (2020). How can we achieve accountability in policing? The (Not-so-secret) ingredients to effective police reform. *SSRN Electronic Journal.* https://doi.org/10.2139/ssrn.3720162.

Willis, J. J. (2013). *Improving Police: What's Craft Got to Do With It? Ideas in American Policing.* Police Foundation.

Willis, J. J. (2022). "Culture eats strategy for breakfast": An in-depth examination of police officer perceptions of body-worn camera implementation and their relationship to policy, supervision, and training. *Criminology and Public Policy*, 1–25. https://doi.org/10.1111/1745-9133.12591.

Willis, J. J., & Mastrofski, S. D. (2017). Understanding the culture of craft: Lessons from two police agencies. *Journal of Crime and Justice, 40*(1), 84–100. https://doi.org/10.1080/0735648x.2016.1174497.

Willis, J. J., & Mastrofski, S. D. (2018). Improving policing by integrating craft and science: What can patrol officers teach us about good police work? *Policing and Society, 28*(1), 27–44.

Willis, J. J., Mastrofski, S. D., & Weisburd, D. L. (2004). Compstat and bureaucracy: A case study of challenges and opportunities for change. *Justice Quarterly, 21*(3), 463–496. https://doi.org/10.1080/07418820400095871.

Willis, J. J., Mastrofski, S. D., & Weisburd, D. (2007). Making sense of COMPSTAT: A theory-based analysis of organizational change in three police departments. *Law & Society Review, 41*(1), 147–188. https://doi.org/10.1111/j.1540-5893.2007.00294.x.

Willis, J. J., & Toronjo, H. (2019). Translating police research into policy: Some implications of the National Academies report on proactive policing for policymakers and researchers. *Police Practice and Research, 20*(6), 617–631. https://doi.org/10.1080/15614263.2019.1657631.

Willis. J. J., Koen, M.K. & Toronjo, H. (2022). Governing police discretion through a craft learning model: Promises and Pitfalls. *European Journal of Policing Studies*, 1-22. doi: 10.5553/EJPS/2034760X2022001005

Willis, J. J. & Toronjo, H. (2023). Exploring a craft learning model for reviewing patrol officer decision-making in encounters with the public. *Law and Social Inquiry*, 48(3), 819-46.

Wilson, J. Q. (1968). *Varieties of Police Behavior*. Harvard University Press.

Wilson, J. Q., & Kelling, G. L. (1982). Broken windows. *The Atlantic Monthly, 249*, 29–38.

Wittgenstein, L. (1958). *Philosophical Investigations*. Translated by Anscombe G.E.M. Basil Blackwell.

Wolfe, S., Rojek, J., McLean, K., & Alpert, G. (2020). Social interaction training to reduce police use of force. *The ANNALS of the American Academy of Political and Social Science, 687*(1), 124–145. https://doi.org/10.1177/0002716219887366.

Worden, R. E., & Dole, C. J. (2019). The holy grail of democratic policing. *Criminal Justice Ethics, 38*(1), 41–54. https://doi.org/10.1080/0731129x.2019.1586217.

Yanow, D., & Tsoukas, H. (2009). What is reflection-in-action? A phenomenological account. *Journal of Management Studies, 46*(8), 1339–1364. https://doi.org/10.1111/j.1467-6486.2009.00859.x.

Zimring, F. E. (2017). *When Police Kill*. Harvard University Press.

Printed in the United States
by Baker & Taylor Publisher Services